Suzuki
500 Twin
Owners
Workshop
Manual

by D J Rabone
B. Tech.

Models covered:
T 500.   492 cc.   UK and USA 1968 to 1975
GT 500 A. 492 cc.   UK and USA 1975 on

ISBN 0 85696 135 3

Printed in the USA   *(135 — 11/1)*

ABCDE
FGHIJ
KLMNO
PQ*

HAYNES PUBLISHING GROUP
SPARKFORD YEOVIL SOMERSET BA22 7JJ ENGLAND
distributed in the USA by
HAYNES PUBLICATIONS INC
861 LAWRENCE DRIVE
NEWBURY PARK
CALIFORNIA 91320
USA

Acknowledgements

Grateful thanks are due to Suzuki (Great Britain) Limited for permission to reproduce their drawings. Brian Horsfall gave the necessary assistance with the dismantling of the T500R used for the photographs in this manual and devised the ingenious methods for overcoming the lack of service tools. Les Brazier arranged and took the photographs; Jeff Clew edited the text and John Murphy originated the layout.

Thanks are also due to Mr Brian Ingle-Finch and the staff of Huxhams (Motor Cycles) Limited, Parkstone, Poole, for the supply of the above machine and also for their kind co-operation in providing information about the T500 series of motor cycles, based on their very extensive knowledge as Suzuki agents.

Final acknowledgements are due to the Avon Rubber Company who kindly supplied the illustrations that apply to tyre fitting.

About this manual

This manual contains a detailed stripdown and replacement procedure for every major assembly of the T500 series of motor cycle. The author advises that where only part of a stripdown is required, the owner should read fully both the relevant stripdown and replacement procedures and decide which parts of the machine he must remove in order to reach his objective, ie if a carburettor overhaul is desired, it is not necessary to remove the engine but it is necessary to remove all the fittings such as the petrol pipes, vacuum pipe inlet and air cleaner ducts and the carburettor top complete with slide and needle.

The author learnt his motor cycle mechanics by 'trial and error' - an expensive and time consuming method. With the help of this manual and a little patience, the owner should find maintaining his own motor cycle an interesting hobby which will save him many pounds in garage fees and spare him the burden of taking his machine to a garage for its routine maintenance.

Unless specially mentioned and therefore considered essential, Suzuki service tools have not been used. There is invariably some alternative means of loosening or slackening some vital component when service tools are not available and risk of damage has to be avoided at all costs.

Each of the six chapters is divided into numbered sections. Within the sections are numbered paragraphs. Cross-reference throughout this manual is quite straightforward and logical. When reference is made 'See Section 6.10' it means Section 6, paragraph 10 in the same Chapter. If another chapter were meant, the text would read 'See Chapter 2, Section 6.10'.

All photographs are captioned with a section/paragraph number to which they refer and are always relevant to the chapter text adjacent.

Figure numbers (usually line illustrations) appear in numerical order, within a given chapter. Fig 1.1 therefore refers to the first figure in Chapter 1. Left hand and right hand descriptions of the machines and their components refer to the left and right of a given machine, when the rider is seated normally.

Motorcycle manufacturers continually make changes to specifications and recommendations, and these, when notified, are incorporated at the earliest opportunity.

Whilst every care is taken to ensure that the information in this manual is correct no liability can be accepted by the authors or publishers for loss, damage or injury caused by any errors in or omissions from the information given.

Modifications to the Suzuki T500 range

Over five years have passed since the first T500 reached the UK market - a period during which design changes and detail improvements have been made. All significant changes are mentioned in the main text. It must be appreciated that some variants of the models included in this manual were supplied to countries other than the UK, but in the main these differences are either 'cosmetic' or relate to the lighting equipment, which has to meet the statutory requirements of the country into which the machine is imported, and the procedures in this manual may be followed with confidence.

Contents

Introduction to the Suzuki 500 range

The Suzuki Motor Company commenced making motor cycles in 1936. However, their machines were not imported to the UK until 1963. Backed by the success of their racing machinery, the 250 cc models quickly caught on and their impressive performance has maintained their popularity.

In November 1968 Suzuki introduced their first 500 cc machine, the T500 Cobra and showed they had overcome the design problems of building a high revving large capacity two-stroke engine. Once again, the performance obtainable from Suzuki's machine immediately took it into the production racing field and it was later developed for road racing - its only apparent drawback being its high fuel consumption which necessitated large fuel tanks for long distance events.

A year after its introduction, the Cobra was revamped and introduced to the UK as the T500 II. This machine, in turn, was discontinued in August 1970 and replaced in October 1970 by the T500 III Charger which possessed a luggage grid on the petrol tank and a few minor modifications. However, in January 1971 the T500 III became the T500R with the disappearance of the luggage grid and the inclusion of a restyled tank and new colour scheme, a tripmeter in the speedometer and a new lighting switch. January 1972 and another paint scheme plus a few minor modifications turned the 'R' to a 'T'; January 1973 brought the T500K and January 1974 the T500L which shows that Suzuki must be well pleased with their T500 series.

In general, the T500 series of motor cycles have been virtually unchanged since the initial revamping of the T500 Cobra. This shows that extensive development work must have been carried out by Suzuki before they introduced the tried and tested machine to the UK. From the maintenance viewpoint, the engine is relatively easy to work on, as are most two-strokes, and should present few problems to the home mechanic. Also,

dealers have indicated that the motor is reliable and rarely requires a complete stripdown as long as regular maintenance has been carried out by the owner. In addition, riders comments must place it as one of the best motor cycles available today - a high performance, finely balanced, well designed machine.

Suzuki have shown that, with their 'Possi-force' (or 'CCI') lubrication system, they can produce reliable, large capacity two-stroke motor cycle engines and, unlike their other Japanese competitors, have remained faithful to the two-stroke for their two and three cylinder machines. Experience gained in the early 1960's under the exacting conditions of racing led to a World Championship; proof enough that Suzuki rank amongst the leaders in the design and manufacture of high performance two-stroke engines. The trend continues, as emphasised by Suzuki's recent victory in the British 'Formula 750' Championship and by the formation of the Suzuki Owners Club of Great Britain.

Dimensions	T500	GT500A
Overall length	86.2 in (2190 mm)	86.9 in (2206 mm)
Overall width	34.3 in (870 mm)	34.6 in (880 mm)
Overall height	44.3 in (1125 mm)	44.7 in (1135 mm)
Wheelbase	57.3 in (1455 mm)	57.7 in (1466 mm)
Ground clearance	6.9 in (175 mm)	6.3 in (160 mm)
Dry weight	412 lb (187 kg)	395 lb (179 kg)

The 1975 Suzuki GT 500A model

Ordering spare parts

When wishing to purchase spare parts for the Suzuki twins, it is best to deal direct with an accredited Suzuki agent or Suzuki (Great Britain) Limited. Either is in the best position to supply ex-stock and have more technical experience in the event of any problems that may arise. When ordering parts, always quote the frame and engine numbers IN FULL, without omitting any prefixes or suffixes.

It is also advisable to take note of the colour scheme, the model designation from the handbook (ie T500, T500 II ... T500K, T500L), and the number stamped on the carburettor top (when requiring carburettor parts).

The engine number is stamped below the lip at the rear of the upper crankcase.

The frame number is stamped along the right hand side of the steering head. There is also a manufacturer's nameplate rivetted to the left hand side of the steering head, on which the corresponding frame and engine numbers are stamped.

Always fit parts of genuine Suzuki manufacture and not pattern parts, which are often available at lower cost. Pattern parts do not necessarily make a satisfactory replacement for the originals and there are many cases where reduced life or sudden failure has occurred, to the detriment of performance.

Some of the more expendable parts such as spark plugs, bulbs, tyres, oils and greases etc., can be obtained from accessory shops and motor factors, who have convenient opening hours, charge lower prices and can often be found not far from home. It is also possible to obtain parts on a Mail Order basis from a number of specialists who advertise regularly in the motor cycle magazines.

Location of engine number

Manufacturer's name plate

Location of frame number

Routine maintenance

Periodic routine maintenance is a continuous process that commences immediately the machine is used and continues until the machine is no longer fit for service. It must be carried out at specified mileage recordings or on a calendar basis if the machine is not used regularly, whichever is the soonest. Maintenance should be regarded as an insurance policy, to help keep the machine in the peak of condition and to ensure long, trouble-free service. It has the additional benefit of giving early warning of any faults that may develop and will act as a safety check, to the obvious advantage of both rider and machine alike.

The various maintenance tasks are described, under their respective mileage and calendar headings. Accompanying diagrams are provided, where necessary. It should be remembered that the interval between the various maintenance tasks serves only as a guide. As the machine gets older, is driven hard or is used under particularly adverse conditions, it is advisable to reduce the period between each check.

Some of the tasks are described in detail, where they are not mentioned fully as a routine maintenance item in the text. If a specific item is mentioned but not described in detail, it will be covered fully in the appropriate chapter. No special tools are required for the normal routine maintenance tasks. The tools contained in the tool kit supplied with every new machine will suffice, but if they are not available, the tools found in the average household will make an adequate substitute.

RM1. TORQUE SETTINGS

No.	Part	Quantity	Tightening Torque
1	Front axle nut	1	650 kg cm (47 lb ft)
2	Fork inner tube fitting bolt	2	200 kg cm (14 lb ft)
3	Steering stem head fitting bolt	3	250 kg cm (18 lb ft)
4	Handlebar clamp bolt	4	130 kg cm (9.5 lb ft)
5	Spark plug	2	200 kg cm (14 lb ft)
6	Cylinder head nut and bolt	16	350 kg cm, 200 kg cm
7	Kickstarter fitting bolt	1	300 kg cm (21 lb ft)
8	Rear shock absorber nut	4	250 kg cm (18 lb ft)
9	Rear axle nut	1	650 kg cm (47 lb ft)
10	Muffler fitting bolt	4	300 kg cm (21 lb ft)
11	Rear swinging arm pivot shaft	1	650 kg cm (47 lb ft)
12	Engine mounting bolt	3	600 kg cm (43 lb ft)
13	Exhaust pipe fitting bolt	4	130 kg cm (9.5 lb ft)
14	Spoke nipple	72	

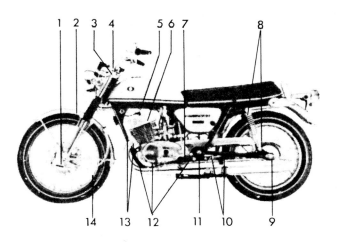

RM1. Torque wrench settings: check regularly

Weekly, or every 200 miles

Check the oil level through the inspection window in the side of the oil tank. If the level is close to or below the centre screw, top up with one of the prescribed oils.

Check the tyre pressures. Always check when the tyres are cold, using a pressure gauge known to be accurate.

Check the level of the electrolyte in the battery. Use only distilled water to top up, unless there has been a spillage of acid. Do not overfill.

Give the whole machine a close visual inspection, checking for loose nuts and fittings, frayed control cables etc. Make sure the lights, horn and traffic indicators function correctly, also the speedometer.

Monthly, or every 750 miles

Complete all the checks listed in the weekly/200 mile service, and then the following:

Check the operation of the oil pump. If necessary, adjust the control lever to correspond with the adjusting marks.

Clean both spark plugs.

Change the oil in the gearbox.

Adjust the play in the throttle and brake cables.

If necessary, adjust the carburettors to ensure smooth running at low rpm.

Check the contact breaker points gaps and verify whether the ignition timing is correct.

Adjust both brakes and also the amount of play in the final drive chain.

Check the tightness of the cylinder head bolts, exhaust pipe clamps and exhaust rear mounting bolts.

Check the steering head bearings for slackness.

Check both wheels for loose or broken spokes.

Check the clutch adjustment.

Three-monthly, or every 2000 miles

Complete all the checks under the weekly and monthly headings, then carry out the following additional tasks:

Remove and clean the oil tank outlet cap and strainer.

Remove, clean and lubricate the final drive chain.

Clean the air filter.

Adjust the gaps of both spark plugs.

Lubricate the contact breaker.

Grease the swinging arm.

Six-monthly, or every 4000 miles

Complete all the checks under the weekly, monthly and three-monthly headings, then attend to the following:

Replace both spark plugs.

Lubricate the throttle, brake and oil pump control cables.

Decarbonise the engine and clean out the exhaust system.

Grease the twist grip throttle.

Clean the oil outlet filter and the fuel tap filter.

Yearly, or every 8000 miles

Again complete all the checks listed under the weekly, monthly, three-monthly and six-monthly headings. The following additional tasks are now necessary:

Dismantle and clean both carburettors.

Replace both sets of contact breaker points.

Remove both wheels and check condition of front and rear brake shoes. Replace, if linings have worn thin.

RM2. Window in oil tank shows level of contents

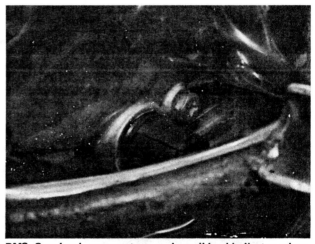

RM3. Crosshead screw acts as gearbox oil level indicator, when removed

RM4. Grease swinging arm using the nipple provided

Quick glance routine maintenance and capacities

Contact breaker gap	0.3 – 0.4 mm (0.012 – 0.016 inch)
Spark plug gap	0.5 – 0.6 mm (0.020 – 0.024 inch)
Spark plug type	NGK B8HS or B7HS (NGK B-77HC original fitment)
Ignition timing	24°BTDC, 3.44 mm (0.134 inch) BTDC
Fuel tank capacity	3.1 Imp gal
Oil tank capacity	1.8 litre
Tyre pressures:	
Solo	Front 23 psi, Rear 27 psi
With pillion	Front 23 psi, Rear 33 psi
Drive chain slack	15 – 20 mm (0.6 – 0.8 inch)

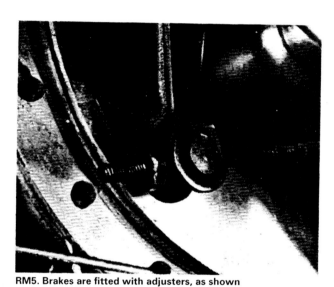

RM5. Brakes are fitted with adjusters, as shown

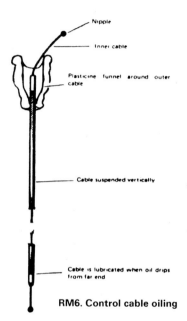

RM6. Control cable oiling

Recommended lubricants

ENGINE	Two-stroke motorcycle oil for injector systems. The oil is contained in a separate tank (1.8 litre capacity) which forms part of the 'Posi-Force' lubrication system. Oil should NOT be mixed with the petrol in the fuel tank.
GEARBOX	10W/40 motor oil. T500 models 1400 cc, GT500A models 1600 cc
GREASE NIPPLES	General purpose grease
CONTROL CABLES	Light oil or aerosol cable lubricant
TELESCOPIC FORKS	10, 15 or 20W fork oil. T500 models 220 cc per leg, GT500A models 266 cc per leg
CHAIN	Aerosol chain lube or engine oil

List of illustrations

Chapter 1 Engine Clutch and Gearbox

Contents

Specifications

Model	All T500 models and GT500A
Engine	Twin cylinder two stroke
Cylinder heads	Aluminium alloy
Cylinder barrels	Aluminium alloy
Bore	70 mm (2.75 in)
Stroke	64 mm (2.52 in)
Cubic capacity	492 cc
Compression ratio (corrected)...	6.6 : 1
Maximum bhp at 7000 rpm	47
Maximum torque at 6000 rpm	37.5 lb ft 38.3 lb ft
Weight	139 lb (63 kg)
Pistons	
Type	Aluminium with piston ring pegs
Oversizes available	+ 0.5 mm (0.020 in), + 1.0 mm (0.040 in)

Piston rings
 Number ... ...   Two per piston
 Gap ... ...   0.008 - 0.040 in
 Groove clearance ... ...   Not greater than 0.006 in
Capacities
 Oil tank ... ...   1.8 litres (3.2 pints)
 Gearbox ... ...   1.2 litres (2.2 pints)
Gear ratios
 Bottom gear ... ...   2.500 : 1
 Second gear ... ...   1.563 : 1
 Third gear ... ...   1.158 : 1
 Fourth gear ... ...   0.955 : 1
 Top gear ... ...   0.870 : 1
 Primary drive ... ...   2.50 : 1
 Final drive (standard) ... ...   2.20 : 1 (33/15)

Overall reduction in top gear ... ... $\dfrac{0.87}{1} \times \dfrac{2.50}{1} \times \dfrac{2.20}{1} = \dfrac{4.79}{1}$

Clutch
 Friction plates
  Number   7
 Thickness
  Standard ... ...   3.5 mm (0.138 in)
  Minimum ... ...   3.2 mm (0.126 in)
 Maximum warpage ... ...   0.4 mm (0.016 in)
 Steel plates
  Number   7
 Thickness
  Standard ... ...   2 mm (0.08 in)
  Minimum ... ...   1.85 mm (0.07 in)
 Maximum warpage ... ...   0.1 mm (0.004 in)

Clutch springs
 Free length
  Standard ... ...   40.4 mm (1.58 in)
  Minimum ... ...   39.0 mm (1.53 in)

Torque wrench settings

	lb ft	kg cm
Cylinder head nuts (long)	25	350
Cylinder head bolts (short)	14.4	200
Engine sprocket nut	29	400
Oil pump union bolt	3.6	50
Primary pinion	36	500
Crankcase bolts - 6 mm...	7	100
Crankcase bolts - 8 mm...	14	200

Miscellaneous
 Backlash in primary drive
  Standard ... ...   0.025 - 0.065 mm
  Maximum ... ...   0.16 mm (0.006 in)
 Maximum crankshaft run-out ... ...   0.06 mm (0.0024 in)
 Maximum sideways play at small end ... ...   3 mm (0.118 in)
 Gear selector fork - gearwheel clearance
  Standard ... ...   0.4 - 0.6 mm
  Maximum ... ...   0.8 mm (0.03 in)
 Clutch housing - axial play
  Standard ... ...   0.05 - 0.20 mm
  Maximum ... ...   0.25 mm (0.01 in)
 Maximum piston clearance ... ...   0.15 mm (0.006 in)

1 General description

The engine/gear unit fitted to the 500 cc Suzuki twins is of the two-stroke type employing flat top pistons and what is known as 'loop scavenging' to achieve a satisfactory induction and exhaust sequence. A rigid built-up crankshaft with thick flywheels ensures good crankcase compression; the shape and arrangement of the ports guarantees a very high standard of performance without need for mechanical aids such as rotary or reed induction valves.

The crankcase assembly is arranged to split horizontally thereby giving maximum access to the engine and gearbox components. In fact, it is not possible to work on the gearbox without first removing the engine from the frame and then splitting the crankcase assembly. This disadvantage of the horizontally-split, unit construction engine should be weighed against the general increase in oil tightness obtained.

The gearbox has five speeds and is fitted with a conventional kickstart. Primary drive is through a pair of helically-cut pinions, via a multi-plate clutch. A positive stop mechanism is incorporated in the gear change system, to ensure each gear is selected with a positive action.

Unlike many other two-strokes, the engine does not rely upon a petrol/oil mix for lubrication. Oil is contained within a separate oil tank, from which it is fed by gravity to a mechanical oil pump interconnected with the throttle. This 'Posi-Force' (later renamed 'CCI') system ensures that oil is delivered under pressure at all times to the crankshaft assembly and to the cylinder walls. The output of the pump is controlled by engine speed (via the throttle linkage) and thus the correct amount of oil is supplied under all operating conditions. The pump has a limited range of adjustment.

The gearbox has its own separate oil content and is fitted with a level plug to prevent accidental overfilling. It holds only a small quantity of oil, which must be changed at the recommended intervals.

2 Operations with the engine/gearbox in the frame

It is not necessary to remove the engine/gear unit from the frame unless the crankshaft assembly and/or the gearbox components require attention. Most operations can be accomplished with the engine in place, such as:
1 Removal and replacement of the cylinder heads.
2 Removal and replacement of the cylinder barrels and pistons.
3 Removal and replacement of the flywheel magneto generator.
4 Removal and replacement of the clutch.

When several operations need to be undertaken simultaneously it would probably be an advantage to remove the complete unit from the frame, a comparatively simple operation that should take approximately thirty minutes. This will give the advantage of better access and more working space.

3 Operations with engine/gearbox removed

1 Removal and replacement of the outboard oil seals.
2 Removal and replacement of the crankshaft assembly.
3 Removal and replacement of the gear clusters, selectors and gearbox main bearings.
4 Renewal of the kickstart return spring.

4 Method of engine/gearbox removal

As described previously, the engine and gearbox are built as a unit and it is necessary to remove the unit complete in order to gain access to either. Separation of the crankcases is accomplished after the engine unit has been removed and refitting cannot take place until the crankcases have been reassembled.

5 Removing the engine/gearbox unit

1 Place the machine on the centre stand and make sure that it is standing firmly. Remove the gearbox drain plugs and drain off the oil, preferably when warm.
2 Make sure the diaphragm-type petrol tap is in the 'ON' position and pull off the two fuel pipes. Remove also the vacuum pipe which connects the left hand carburettor flange with the petrol tap diaphragm.
3 Disconnect the electrical leads from the battery at the snap connectors and remove the battery; these parts are situated behind the battery cover on the left hand side behind the air filter.
4 Disconnect the alternator wires by pulling them apart at the socket connector and the other snap connector joints: these are also situated in the battery box, to the rear of the battery. Note the wires are colour-coded to make reconnection easy.
5 Remove the seat by loosening the bolts through the rearmost lugs of the top frame tube and pulling the seat back and up. This operation exposes a large bolt at the back of the petrol tank; unscrew this bolt from the frame and the tank may now be removed. The tank rests on rubber mats at the rear and rubber stops at the front; do not lose these or the tank will vibrate against the frame when the engine is running.

6 The exhaust systems may be removed as complete units. Unscrew both the bolts which hold each exhaust pipe clamp to the barrels. Also remove the rear (pillion) footrests and neighbouring bolts; these act as the rear support for the exhaust system. During this operation, the exhaust system will drop on the ground unless supported. Note that the exhaust pipes are a sliding fit in the silencers.
7 Detach the clutch outer cable from the handlebar lever in order to gain sufficient slack for the other end to be later removed from the engine sprocket cover.
8 Remove the final drive chain by detaching the spring link. This task is made easier if the spring link is located on the rear wheel sprocket.
9 Unscrew the tachometer drive cable connection at the top of the oil pump cover, and pull the cable end free. Remove the outer oil pump cover (two bolts) and remove the throttle cable linkage. Note that the cable has a detachable nipple - do not lose. Unscrew the cable from the cable stop.
10 Detach the flexible plastic pipe from the bottom of the oil tank by removing the union bolt. To prevent the oil content escaping from the tank, screw a 6 mm bolt into the union joint, to act as a temporary plug - a crosshead screw from the outer engine covers is suitable.
11 Pull off both spark plug caps complete with leads and secure them away from the engine.
12 Remove both carburettor tops by unscrewing each screwed ring. The tops can be lifted away complete with their control cables, springs and throttle slide assemblies. Care is necessary at this stage to prevent damage to the slides or the needles suspended from them. Tape each top and slide assembly to a convenient frame tube, so that they are out of harm's way when the engine is lifted out.
13 Remove the air cleaner hoses from each carburettor intake by undoing the crosshead screws which tighten the retaining clips. A third clip at the air cleaner box now holds the rubber duct; loosen the screw and remove the duct. Although not strictly necessary, better access for engine removal is gained if the air filter box is removed too. This is retained at the back and the front by two small nuts and screws.
14 Pull off the electrical connections to the rear brake stop lamp switch. Remove the operating spring and then loosen the plate retaining bolt and remove the switch unit.
15 Disconnect the rear brake cable from the lever by removing the split pin and clevis pin.
16 Remove both forward footrests by unscrewing the two bolts which screw into the bosses on the frame; disconnect the rear brake lever return spring and pull off the lever (right hand side).
17 Remove COMPLETELY the pinch bolts which hold the kickstart and gear change levers on their respective splined shafts. Pull off the levers and inspect the splines for wear. Note: The gear change shaft goes right through the engine unit thus a right hand gear change conversion may be made.
18 The rear left hand engine cover (the final drive sprocket cover) is retained by six crosshead screws. Remove these and pull off the cover complete with clutch cable; the cover also contains the clutch actuating mechanism. Disconnect the clutch cable nipple noting that it is retained by a bent over tab. Unscrew the outer cable from the cover.
19 Remove the screw and bolt which attach the chainguard to the swinging arm and lift out the chainguard.
20 There are now only the three large engine bolts to be removed. Unscrew the nuts and pull out the bolts slowly, allowing the engine to settle ¼ inch onto the bottom frame loop; note the position of the spacer on the rear engine bolt.
21 The engine unit is heavy (139 lbs) and so the removal is a two-man job. Pick up the engine in a straight lift and move out to the left, when clear of the engine mounting lugs.

6 Dismantling the engine and gearbox - general

1 Before commencing work on the engine unit, the external surfaces must be cleaned thoroughly. A motor cycle engine has

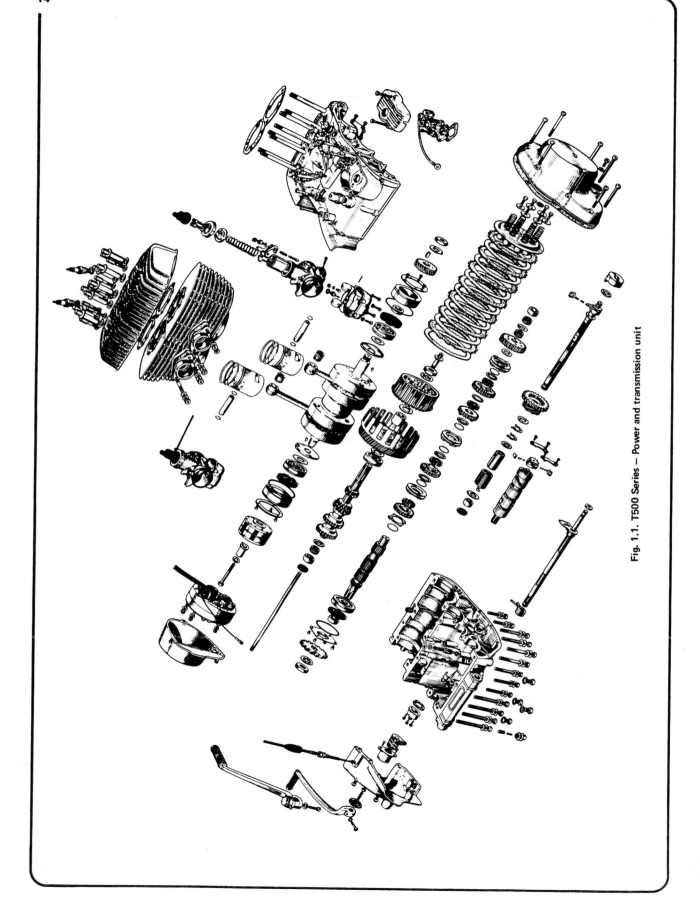

Fig. 1.1. T500 Series — Power and transmission unit

5.3 Disconnect the battery leads at the snap connector

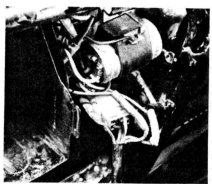

5.4 Disconnect the alternator wires from the large snap connector and the other single snap connectors

5.5 Bolts through the rearmost lugs of the top frame tube retain the seat

5.6a Remove the bolts which retain the exhaust pipe clamp to the barrels

5.6b Rear footrest and neighbouring bolt act as rear support for the exhaust system

5.9 Throttle cable linkage shown removed. The nipple is detachable

5.10 An engine cover screw may be used to blank the union

5.12 Screw cap and slide assembly should be removed complete

5.14a Pull off the leads from the brake light switch

5.14b Disconnect the brake light spring and rear brake cable

5.17 Ease kickstart lever, with pinchbolt completely removed off its splines

5.18 Pull off the final drive cover complete with clutch cable

5.20 Use a Mole Wrench to extract the engine bolts — NEVER hammer the threaded ends to remove bolts or damage to the threads may occur

5.21 Lift out the engine from the left hand side

very little protection from road grit and other foreign matter, which will sooner or later find its way into the dismantled engine if this simple precaution is not observed.

2 One of the proprietary engine cleaning compounds such as Gunk or Jizer can be used to good effect, especially if the compound is allowed to penetrate the film of oil and grease before it is washed away. When washing down, make sure that water cannot enter the carburettors or the electrical system, particularly if these parts are now more exposed.

3 Never use force to remove any stubborn part, unless mention is made of this requirement in the text. There is invariably good reason why a part is difficult to remove, often because the dismantling operation has been tackled in the wrong sequence.

4 Dismantling will be made easier if a simple engine stand is constructed that will correspond with the engine mounting points. This arrangement will permit the complete unit to be clamped rigidly to the workbench, leaving both hands free for the dismantling operation.

7 Dismantling the engine and gearbox - removing the carburettors

1 The carburettors may be removed before or after engine removal by loosening the crosshead screws in the retaining clips around the rubber inlet manifolds and pulling out the carburettor

bodies.

2 Place the carburettors aside for further attention. They are easily damaged or broken if they receive harsh treatment. If required they can be separated by withdrawing the split pin from the end of the rod which operates both chokes in unison.

3 Remove the nuts and washers holding the inlet manifolds to the cylinder barrels. Pull off the manifolds and the heat resistant gaskets.

7.1 Pull the carburettor bodies from the rubber inlet manifold and remove as a pair

8 Dismantling the engine and gearbox - removing the cylinder heads and barrels

1 Each cylinder has its own separate cylinder head. To remove each head, unscrew the cylinder head retaining nuts and bolts in a diagonal sequence, to prevent distortion.

2 When the nuts and bolts have been slackened fully and withdrawn, each cylinder head can be lifted off the long retaining studs which pass through each cylinder barrel. Note that an aluminium cylinder head gasket is used to seal the cylinder head to the barrel joint. These should be discarded and not re-used, even if they appear to be in good condition.

3 Each of the separate cylinder barrels can now be lifted off by drawing them upwards along the holding down studs. Take care to support each piston as it falls clear of the cylinder barrel, otherwise the piston may be damaged or the rings broken. If only a 'top' overhaul is contemplated, it is advisable to pad the mouth of each crankcase with clean rag before the pistons are drawn clear of the cylinder barrel. This will prevent particles of broken piston ring (or displaced circlips from the next stage of the dismantling procedure) from dropping into the crankcase and causing further unnecessary dismantling.

4 Remove and discard the cylinder base gaskets which will also have to be renewed.

9 Dismantling the engine and gearbox - removing the pistons and piston rings

1 Remove both circlips from each piston boss and discard them. Circlips should never be re-used if risk of displacement is to be obviated.

2 Using a drift of the correct diameter, tap each gudgeon pin out of the piston bosses until the piston complete with rings can be lifted off the connecting rod. Make sure the piston is properly supported during this operation, to prevent the connecting rod from bending.

3 If the gudgeon pin is a tight fit, the piston should first be warmed in order to expand the gudgeon pin bosses. A convenient way of warming the piston is to place a rag soaked in hot water on the crown.

4 When the pistons have been detached from the connecting rods, mark them on the inside of the skirt so that they will be replaced in the barrel from which they came. Note that the pistons are not identical and that the ports in the barrels and pistons will not align if the pistons are interchanged. There is no need to mark the back and front because each piston has an arrow cast in the crown, which must always face the front of the machine.

5 The small end bearings take the form of caged needle rollers. Each roller assembly will lift out of the connecting rod eye.

6 Note that the piston rings are pegged so that they will remain in a set location. This is important, otherwise the rings will rotate whilst the engine is running, permitting the ends to become trapped in the ports and broken.

7 To remove the rings spread the ends sufficiently with the thumbs to allow each ring to be lifted clear of the piston. This is a very delicate operation which must be handled with great care. Piston rings are brittle and they break very easily.

8 If the rings are stuck in their grooves or have become gummed by oily deposits, it is sometimes possible to free them by working small strips of tin along the back to give a 'peeling' action.

10 Dismantling the engine and gearbox - removing the alternator

1 Remove the alternator cover (the front left hand engine cover) by undoing the three crosshead screws.

2 Also remove the small plate within the outer half of the crankcase which holds the rubber grommet through which the generator leads pass. It is located in the top right hand side of the alternator compartment and is retained by a single crosshead screw. When this plate is removed, and the cable retaining clips (along the top of the crankcase) are slackened, the stator plate assembly complete with wiring harness can be detached. It is necessary to remove the three crosshead screws which retain the stator plate, complete with contact breaker assemblies, to the left hand crankcase. There is sufficient clearance for the large terminal connector to pass through the hole in the outer crankcase once the rubber grommet is removed.

3 To remove the flywheel rotor, lock the engine by passing a stout metal rod through the eyes of the connecting rods so that it rests across the crankcase mouth, and is supported by two short lengths of wood. Slacken the centre bolt of the rotor (right hand thread) and if the appropriate Suzuki extractor is not available, use a three-legged sprocket puller as shown in the accompanying photograph. Excessive force should not be necessary to break the taper joint. Tighten the sprocket puller until it is hard up against the slackened centre bolt and then give a smart hammer blow on the end of the puller. The rotor can now be withdrawn when the centre bolt is removed completely and the Woodruff key placed in a safe place until it is required for reassembly. Note that the contact breaker cam will also be freed when the centre bolt is removed. Its position is pre-determined by a dowel pin which engages with the rotor keyway.

4 It is advisable at this stage to also remove the final drive sprocket which is retained by a nut and tab washer. Once again, lock the engine with the gearbox 'in gear', flatten the tab washer and undo the nut which has a right hand thread. Pull off the sprocket.

11 Dismantling the engine and gearbox - removing the clutch

1 Working from the right hand side of the engine unit, first remove the outer cover. This is held in place by nine crosshead screws which are often very tight and may require the use of an impact screwdriver. Make provision for catching any surplus oil which may drain away when the cover is removed. Note that the two long screws pass through spacers seated in the crankcase - remove the spacers and keep them safe, if loose. Before the cover may be removed, the plastic cover over the end of the gear change shaft must be pulled off. Use a wooden drift to ease it off if

necessary. Never use a screwdriver to lever off alloy casings.

2 Remove the gasket.

3 Lock the engine again and withdraw completely the six clutch spring bolts. The clutch pressure plate will now lift off and expose the seven plain and seven friction plates which make up the clutch assembly. These plates align with the clutch inner and outer drums respectively and can be prised out of position. Lift out the clutch pushrod end piece which fits within the hollow gearbox mainshaft and also the main clutch pushrod from the left hand end of the mainshaft.

4 With the engine still locked by the bar through the small end, lock the inner and outer clutch bodies together (known as 'spragging the clutch'). The clutch centre may now be removed by undoing the central large nut (which is retained by a tab washer) from the end of the gearbox layshaft. This nut has a right hand thread.

5 Having removed the clutch centre, pull off the washer, the clutch outer (with driven pinion) and the second thrust washer from the mainshaft. Note the positions of the washers.

12 Removing the oil pump assembly

1 Undo the three banjo bolts which retain the oil inlet and the two oil outlet pipes to the pump body.

2 The oil pump is held to the crankcase by two crosshead screws - one either side. Remove these screws and pull off the pump body and gasket.

3 The pump is driven from the gearbox via a shaft with a worm drive. This shaft is exposed on removing the pump - pull out the shaft to avoid it dropping out when the crankcase is later inverted.

13 Separating the crankcases

1 Before the crankcases can be separated, a further amount of preparatory work has to be undertaken.

2 Remove the crankshaft pinion by first flattening the tab washer and undoing the nut (right hand thread) with the engine locked. The pinion is retained by a Woodruff key on a parallel shaft and may require a sprocket puller to ease it off. Also, remove the spacer behind the pinion.

3 Remove the bearing retainer which is immediately behind the mainshaft. An impact screwdriver will be required for this operation.

4 Pull out the gear change selecting shaft, complete with quadrant, from the right hand side of the engine. Note the spacer over the shaft in the engine sprocket compartment.

5 The oil seal support around the final drive shaft is retained by four crosshead screws which will also require an impact screwdriver to slacken them. Pull off the seal support.

6 Remove the neutral switch lead by unscrewing the small crosshead screw from the neutral switch. This unit is located in front and below the gearbox final drive shaft.

7 The crankcases are now ready for separation. Invert the engine and remove the 16 bolts (13 on earlier models) holding the crankcases together. Also remove the two gearchange cam retaining bolts (in front of the gearbox drain plug) if required.

8 Reinvert the engine and remove the last four bolts in the upper half which retain the crankcases together. One of these is located close to the oil pump cable adjuster, which must be withdrawn before the bolt can be released.

9 A few light taps with a rawhide mallet on the projecting portions of the crankcases should ensure the crankcases separate, leaving the remainder of the engine and gearbox components in the lower half.

10 Lift out the gearbox mainshaft and layshaft complete, noting the 'C' ring locaters for the journal bearings.

11 Remove the central crosshead screw and clip which retains the kickstart shaft and lift out the kickstart assembly; as the screw is undone, the shaft will rise because of the tension in the kickstart spring.

8.2 Remove the cylinder head complete with long 'nuts' and short bolts

8.3 Pull the barrels off individually

9.1 Remove the gudgeon pin circlips

9.2 Tap out the gudgeon pin and remove the piston complete with rings

10.2a Remove the rubber grommet which holds the alternator wires

10.2b Pull off the stator plate

10.3a Lock the engine and slacken the rotor retaining bolt one turn

10.3b Use a sprocket puller to remove the rotor

11.3a Remove completely the six clutch spring bolts and washers

11.3b Lift out the pressure plate and fourteen clutch plates

11.3c Remove the clutch pushrod end piece

11.4 'Spragging' the clutch with a metal plate

12.1 Remove the oil inlet union and the two oil outlet unions

13.3 Remove the bearing retainer which is immediately behind the gearbox mainshaft

13.4 Pull out the gearchange shaft and quadrant

13.5 Pull off the final-drive shaft seal support after removing the four screws

13.9 From the top - kickstart shaft, final drive shaft and main-shaft

13.12a Remove the cam retaining plate ...

13.12b ... and striker plate. Note the blanking plug/gearchange stop immediately behind the cam end

13.15 Remove the neutral switch cover and the central contact

12 Unscrew two of and pull out the third oil spray guides.

13 Remove the gearchange striker plate and cam retainer using an impact screwdriver.

14 Pull off the selector pawls - note that the ratchet assembly is operated by four small spring and plunger assemblies which will drop out on release.

15 Remove the blanking plug and pull out the selector rod, noting the relative positions of each selector fork for replacement purposes.

16 Remove the neutral switch cover (two crosshead screws) and the crosshead screw and contact in the end of the gearchange cam. If the two guide bolts have been removed, the cam will slide out through the right hand side of the crankcase.

17 Lift out the crankshaft assembly complete. Once again, note the positions of the 'C' ring and also the dowel pins which locate the main bearings to the crankcase.

14 Removing the crankshaft and gearbox main bearings

1 Before the crankshaft outer main bearings can be removed, it is first necessary to remove the outer oil seals. These are a push fit on the crankshaft and are quite easily withdrawn once the circlips are removed. A special puller is needed to remove the outer main bearings without risk of damage to the crankshaft assembly, although it is possible to use a sprocket puller with thin jaws since there is a thrust washer between each bearing and the nearest flywheel, which provides the necessary clearance.

2 Generally speaking, it is preferable to service exchange the entire crankshaft assembly if any of the bearings are suspect. If the two outer bearings need replacing, it is highly probable that the centre bearing will be in the same condition. It is quite beyond the means of the home mechanic, or for that matter, the majority of motor cycle repair specialists, to separate and re-align the crankshaft assembly without the appropriate equipment. In consequence, the Suzuki Service Exchange Scheme will provide a completely reconditioned crankshaft assembly together with new main bearings, small end bearings and oil seals for a fixed sum, in exchange for the crankshaft which requires attention. Any accredited Suzuki dealer should be able to provide this facility, often ex-stock.

3 By way of explanation, the crankshaft assembly can be regarded as two quite independent flywheel assemblies, coupled together by a 'middle' crankshaft which presses into the inner flywheels. The middle crankshaft carries the centre main bearing and also the two innermost oil seals. The two separate flywheel assemblies are built up first, aligned and checked for run-out. They are then coupled together by the middle crankshaft and the entire assembly is checked for run-out at both ends. It follows that a very high standard of accuracy has to be observed, in order to preserve the smooth running of the engine.

4 The gearbox assembly has an oil seal, located immediately behind the final drive sprocket, on the final drive shaft. This will pull off the shaft without difficulty. The final drive shaft has a large diameter journal ball bearing at the left hand or drive side end and a caged needle roller bearing on the right hand end. The reverse applies in the case of the mainshaft; the journal ball bearing is on the right and the caged needle roller bearing on the left. There should be no difficulty in pulling these bearings off the shafts.

15 Dismantling the gear clusters

1 It should not be necessary to dismantle either of the gear clusters unless damage has occurred to any of the pinions or if the caged needle roller bearings require attention.

2 The accompanying illustration shows how both clusters of the five speed gearbox are assembled on their respective shafts. It is imperative that the gear clusters, including the thrust washers, are assembled in EXACTLY the correct sequence, otherwise constant gear selection problems will occur.

3 In order to eliminate the risk of misplacement, make rough sketches as the clusters are dismantled. Also strip and rebuild as soon as possible to reduce any confusion which might occur at a later date.

16 Examination and renovation - general

1 Before examining the parts of the dismantled engine unit for wear, it is essential that they should be cleaned thoroughly. Use a paraffin/petrol mix to remove all traces of old oil and sludge which may have accumulated within the engine.

2 Examine the crankcase castings for cracks or other signs of damage. If a crack is discovered, it will require professional repair.

3 Examine carefully each part to determine the extent of wear, checking with the tolerance figures listed in the Specifications section of this Chapter. If there is any question of doubt, play safe and renew.

4 Use a clean, lint-free rag for cleaning and drying the various components. This will obviate the risk of small particles obstructing the internal oilways, causing the lubrication system to fail.

17 Big end and main bearings - examination and renovation

1 Failure of the big end bearings is invariably accompanied by a knock within the crankcase which progressively becomes worse.

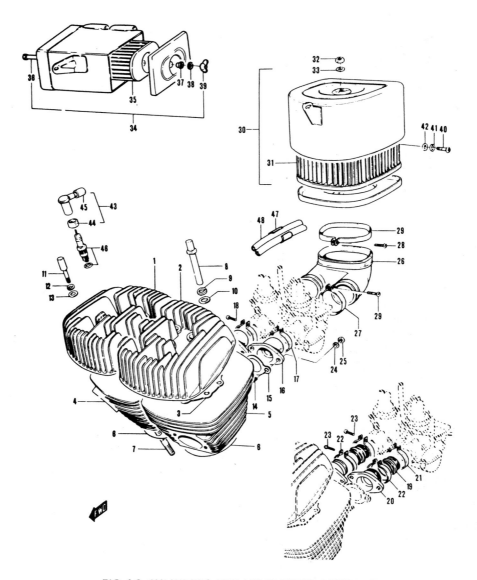

FIG. 1.2. CYLINDERS AND AIR CLEANER ASSEMBLY

1	RH cylinder head
2	LH cylinder head
3	Cylinder head gasket (2 off)
4	RH cylinder barrel
5	LH cylinder barrel
6	Cylinder base gasket (2 off)
7	Cylinder retaining stud (8 off)
8	Cylinder head nut (8 off)
9	Spring washer (8 off)
10	Washer (8 off)
11	Cylinder head bolt (8 off)
12	Spring washer (8 off)
13	Washer (8 off)
14	Inlet manifold stud (4 off)
15	Inlet manifold gasket (2 off)
16	Inlet manifold (2 off)
17	Clamp (2 off)
18	Screw (2 off)
19	Inlet manifold * (2 off)
20	Inlet manifold * (2 off)
21	Clamp * (2 off)
22	Clamp * (2 off)
23	Clamp screw * (4 off)
24	Spring washer (4 off)
25	Nut (4 off)

26	Air cleaner duct
27	Clamp (2 off)
28	Clamp
29	Clamp screw (3 off)
30	Air cleaner assembly
31	Air filter
32	Nut
33	Washer
34	Air cleaner assembly *
35	Air filter *
36	Bolt *
37	Seal *
38	Washer *
39	Butterfly nut *
40	Screw (2 off)
41	Spring washer (2 off)
42	Washer (2 off)
43	Spark plug cap assembly (2 off)

* Post T500J only.

44	Plug cap seal (2 off)
45	Plug cap seal/HT lead seal (2 off)
46	Spark plug assembly (2 off)
47	Clip - overflow hose
48	Overflow hose (2 off)

Some vibration will also be experienced.

2   There should be no vertical play whatsoever in the big end bearings, after the oil has been washed out. If even a small amount of vertical play is evident, the bearings are due for replacement. (A small amount of end float is both necessary and acceptable). Do not continue to run the machine with worn big end bearings, for there is risk of breaking the connecting rods or crankshaft.

3   The built-up nature of the crankshaft assembly precludes the possibility of repair, as mentioned earlier. It will be necessary to obtain a replacement crankshaft assembly complete, under the Suzuki Service Exchange Scheme.

4   Failure of the main bearings is usually evident in the form of an audible rumble from the bottom of the engine, accompanied by vibration which is felt through the footrests.

5   The crankshaft main bearings are of the journal ball type. If wear is evident in the form of play, or if the bearings feel rough as they are rotated, replacement is necessary. Always check after the old oil has been washed out of the bearings. Whilst it is possible to remove the outer bearings at each end of the crankshaft, it is probable that the centre bearing will also require attention. Here again, it will be necessary to obtain a replacement crankshaft assembly, under the Suzuki Service Exchange Scheme.

6   Failure of both the big end bearings and the main bearings may not necessarily occur as the result of high mileage covered. If the machine is used only infrequently, it is possible that condensation within the engine may cause premature bearing failure. The condition of the flywheels is usually the best guide. When condensation troubles have occurred, the flywheels will rust and become discoloured.

18 Oil seals - examination and renovation

1   The crankshaft oil seals form one of the most critical parts in any two-stroke engine because they perform the dual function of preventing oil from leaking along the crankshaft and preventing air from leaking into the crankcase when the incoming mixture is under crankcase compression.

2   Oil seal failure is difficult to define precisely, although in most cases the machine will become difficult to start, particularly when warm. The engine will also tend to run unevenly and there will be a marked fall-off in performance, especially in the higher gears. This is caused by the intake of air into the crankcases which dilutes the mixture whilst it is under crankcase compression, giving an exceptionally weak mixture for ignition.

3   It is possible to renew the outer crankcase oil seals without difficulty, but the inner seals form part of the crankshaft assembly. In this latter case, a replacement crankshaft assembly is the only way of ensuring a satisfactory crankcase seal.

4   It is unusual for the crankcase seals to become damaged during normal service, but instances have occurred when particles of broken piston rings have fallen into the crankcases and lacerated the seals. A defect of this nature will immediately be obvious.

19 Cylinder barrels - examination and renovation

1   The usual indication of badly worn cylinder barrels and pistons is excessive smoking from the exhausts and piston slap, a metallic rattle which occurs when there is little or no load on the engine. If the top of the bore of the cylinder barrels is examined carefully, it will be found that there is a ridge on the thrust side, the depth of which will vary according to the rate of wear which has taken place. This marks the limit of travel of the uppermost piston ring.

2   Measure the bore diameter just below the ridge, using an internal micrometer, or a dial gauge. Compare this reading with the diameter at the bottom of the cylinder bore, which has not been subjected to wear. If the difference in readings exceeds 0.05 mm (0.002 inch) the cylinder should be rebored and fitted with an oversize piston and rings.

3   If a measuring instrument is not available, the amount of cylinder bore wear can be measured by inserting the piston without rings so that it is approximately ¾ inch from the top of the bore. If it is possible to insert a 0.006 inch feeler gauge between the piston and the cylinder wall on the thrust side of the piston, remedial action must be taken.

4   Suzuki provide pistons in two oversizes: 0.5 mm (0.020 inch) and 1.0 mm (0.040 inch).

5   Check that the surface of the cylinder bores is free from score marks or other damage that may have resulted from an earlier engine seizure or a displaced gudgeon pin. A rebore will be necessary to remove any deep indentations, irrespective of the amount of bore wear that has taken place. If the 1 mm overbore does remove all scratches and ridges from the bore, a new barrel is required otherwise a compression leak will occur.

6   Make sure the external cooling fins of the cylinder barrels are not clogged with oil or road dirt, which will otherwise prevent the free flow of air and cause the engine to overheat. Remove any carbon that has accumulated in the exhaust ports, using a blunt-ended scraper so that the surface of the ports is not scratched. Finish off with metal polish so that the ports have a smooth, shiny appearance. This will aid gas flow and prevent carbon from adhering so firmly on future occasions.

7   Under no circumstances modify or re-profile the ports in the search for extra performance. The size and location of the ports is critical in terms of engine performance and the dimensions chosen have been selected to give good performance consistent with a high standard of mechanical reliability.

8   If the cylinder barrels have been rebored, it will be necessary to round off the extreme edges of the ports, to prevent rapid wear of the piston rings. Use a scraper or hand grinder and finish off with fine emery cloth.

20 Pistons and piston rings - examination and renovation

1   If a rebore is necessary, the existing pistons and piston rings can be disregarded because they will have to be replaced with their new oversize equivalents as a matter of course.

2   Remove all traces of carbon from the piston crowns, using a blunt-ended scraper to avoid scratching the surface. Finish off by polishing the crowns with metal polish, so that carbon will not adhere so readily in the future. Never use emery cloth on the soft aluminium.

3   Piston wear usually occurs at the skirt or lower end of the piston and takes the form of vertical streaks or score marks on the thrust face. There may also be some variation in the thickness of the skirt, in an extreme case.

4   The piston ring grooves may have become enlarged in use, allowing the rings to have greater side float. If the clearance exceeds 0.006 inch, the pistons are due for replacement. It is unusual for this amount of wear to occur on its own.

5   Piston ring wear is measured by removing the rings from the piston and inserting them in the cylinder, using the crown of a piston to locate them about 1½ inches from the top of the bore. Make sure they rest square in the bore. Measure the end gap with a feeler gauge; if the gap exceeds 0.040 inch the rings must be replaced (standard gap 0.008 inch to 0.014 inch). When refitting new piston rings, it is also necessary to measure the ring gap. If the gap is too small, the rings will break while the engine is running and cause extensive damage. The ring gap may be increased by filing the ends of the rings with a fine file. Never hold the rings in a vice for this operation - hold the ring in one hand and the file in the other. Support the ring as much as possible by placing the fingers as near the end of the ring as possible and only remove small amounts of metal before rechecking the gap.

6   All machines are fitted with Keystone rings, which can be identified by their shape. These rings are not interchangeable with the conventional type of rings and must be used only in conjunction with Keystone pistons. They have a 7° taper on their uppermost surface. They are handled in the same fashion as conventional rings.

Note: Keystone rings are designed to cut down carbon build-up on the rings; this helps to lessen groove wear and 'gumming'. Also, their shape is such that compression holds the ring tighter against the barrel than conventional rings, making them more efficient in containing the hot gases above the piston.

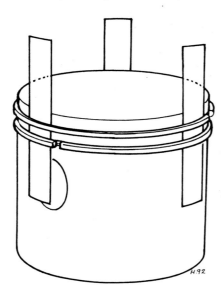

Fig. 1.3. Freeing gummed rings

21 Cylinder heads - examination and renovation

1 Remove all traces of carbon from both cylinder heads, using a blunt-ended scraper. Finish by polishing with metal polish, to give a smooth, shiny surface. This will aid gas flow and will also prevent carbon from adhering so firmly in the future.
2 Check the condition of the threads in the spark plug holes. If the threads are worn or stretched as the result of over-tightening the plugs, they can be reclaimed by a Helicoil thread insert. Most dealers have the means of providing this cheap but effective repair.
3 Make sure the cylinder head fins are not clogged with oil or road dirt, otherwise the engine will overheat. If necessary, use a wire brush to clean the cooling fins.
4 Lay each cylinder head on a sheet of plate glass to check for distortion. Aluminium alloy cylinder heads will distort very easily, especially if the cylinder head bolts are tightened down unevenly. If the amount of distortion is only slight, it is permissible to rub the head down until it is flat once again by wrapping a sheet of very fine emery cloth around the plate glass sheet and rubbing with a rotary motion.
5 If either of the cylinder heads is distorted badly, it is advisable to fit a new replacement. Although the head joint can be restored by skimming in a lathe, this will raise the compression ratio of the engine and may adversely affect performance.

22 Gearbox components - examination and renovation

1 Give the gearbox components a close visual inspection for signs of wear or damage such as broken or chipped teeth, worn dogs, damaged or worn splines and bent selectors. Replace any parts found unserviceable because they cannot be reclaimed in a satisfactory manner.
2 Check the condition of the various pawl springs and the kickstart return spring. If the latter spring fails after the engine has been rebuilt, a further complete stripdown of the engine unit will be necessary.

3 Check the condition of the internal serrations in the kickstart pinion. If these serrations become worn or the edges rounded, the kickstart will slip. Replacement of the pinion is the only means of restoring the full action.
4 Check also that the tip of the kickstart pawl is not worn because this too will promote slip during engagement. If the kickstart pinion is renewed, it is good policy to renew also the pawl.
5 Make sure that the pawl plunger is in good shape and is free from any 'flats'. If in doubt, renew.

23 Clutch - examination and renovation

1 Cork is used as the friction material in the friction clutch plates. When the inserts become worn, the clutch will slip, even if clutch adjustment is correct.
2 Each inserted plate should have a thickness of 3.5 mm (0.138 inch). The wear limit is 3.2 mm (0.126 inch). If the plates have reached the wear limit, they must be replaced.
3 Measure the free length of each clutch spring, because they will take a permanent set after an extended period of service. The free length of a new spring is 40.4 mm (1.58 inch). Replace ALL the clutch springs if any spring has reached the serviceable limit of 39.0 mm (1.53 inch).
4 Check also that none of the plates, either plain or friction, is buckled. Replacement will be necessary if the plates do not lie flat, since it is difficult to straighten them with any success. See the Specifications for acceptable warpage.
5 Check for burrs on the protruding tongues of the inserted plates and/or slots worn in the edges of the outer drum with which they engage. Wear of this nature will cause clutch drag and other troubles, since the plates will not free fully when the clutch is withdrawn. A small amount of wear can be treated by dressing with a file; more extensive wear will necessitate replacement of the parts concerned.
6 If the machine has covered a considerable mileage, it is possible that play will develop in the clutch housing, producing a mysterious rattle in the region of the clutch. This play develops in the axial direction and can be checked by pulling and pushing on the clutch. It can be reduced by grinding down one end of the spacer bush on which the clutch outer drum seats, taking care to remove only a little at a time.
7 Check that the clutch operating mechanism in the final drive cover works quite freely. The mechanism operates on the quick start worm principle.
8 Check the rivets in the clutch outer drum. If they are loose, a new drum is required.

24 Engine and gearbox reassembly - general

1 Before reassembly is commenced, the various engine and gearbox components should be thoroughly clean and placed close to the working area.
2 Make sure all traces of old gaskets have been removed and that the mating surfaces are clean and undamaged. One of the best ways to remove old gasket cement, which is needed only on the crankcase and cover joints, is to apply a rag soaked in methylated spirit. This acts as a solvent and will ensure the cement is removed without resort to scraping and the consequent risk of damage.
3 Gather together all the necessary tools and have available an oil can filled with clean engine oil. Make sure all the new gaskets and oil seals are available; there is nothing more frustrating than having to stop in the middle of a reassembly sequence because a vital gasket or replacement has been overlooked.
4 Make sure the reassembly area is clean and well lit, with adequate working space. Refer to the torque and clearance settings wherever they are given. Many of the smaller bolts are easily sheared if they are over-tightened. Always use the correct size screwdriver bit for the crosshead screws and NEVER an ordinary screwdriver or punch.

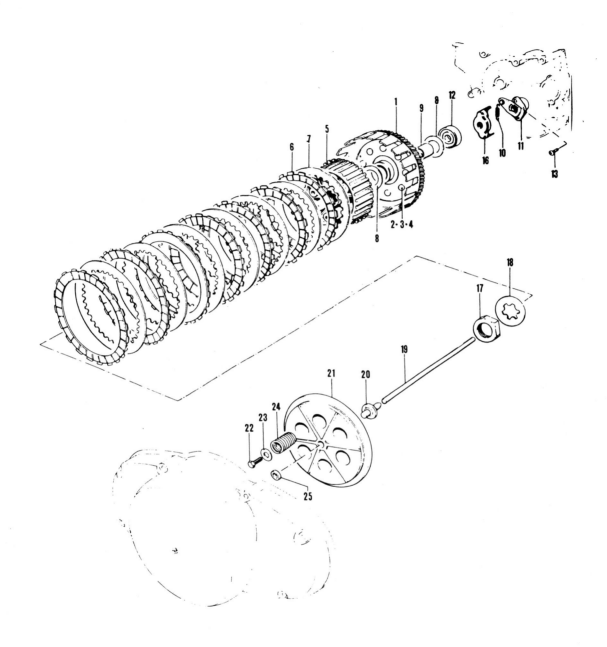

FIG. 1.4. CLUTCH ASSEMBLY

1	Primary driven gear assembly	14	Nut
2	Shock absorber (8 off)	15	Clutch adjusting screw
3	Backplate	16	Clutch release mechanism cover
4	Rivet (8 off)	17	Inner drum retaining nut
5	Inner clutch drum	18	Tab washer
6	Clutch plate - plain (7 off)	19	Clutch push-rod
7	Clutch plate - friction (7 off)	20	Pushrod end piece
8	Thrust washer (2 off)	21	Clutch spring bolt (6 off)
9	Clutch drum spacer	22	Clutch spring bolt (6 off)
10	Spring	23	Washer (6 off)
11	Clutch release worm drive assembly	24	Clutch spring (6 off)
12	Pushrod oil seal	25	Pushrod end piece oil seal
13	Screw (2 off)		

25 Engine and gearbox reassembly - rebuilding the gearbox

1 Place the lower crankcase on the workbench and commence operations by replacing the gear change cam oil seal in the outer, left hand side of the crankcase.
2 Reassemble the ratchet assembly in the end of the gearchange cam and slide the cam into position from the right hand side of the crankcase.
3 Invert the crankcase and insert the gearchange cam guide (solid bolt) in the clutch side of the crankcase. Also replace the gearchange cam stop ensuring that the spring and plunger assembly is free to move easily. Both these bolts should have new washers to ensure a good oil seal.
4 Re-invert the crankcase and slide the gear selector fork rod through the right hand side - locate each fork on the rod and in the cam in EXACTLY the same order as they were removed - push the rod home and screw in the retaining plug (gearchange stop) and washer.
5 Replace the 'C' rings for the location of the mainshaft and final drive shaft journal bearings.
6 Offer up the final drive shaft gear assembly to the selector forks ensuring that the fork ends mate up with the gear selector wheels and also that the journals are properly seated.
7 Slide in the rear oil splash plate. Subsequently, offer up the main shaft assembly so that the gears engage with the drive shaft and the journals are properly seated.

25.1 Replace the gearchange cam oil seal in the lower crankcase half

26 Engine and gearbox reassembly - kickstart replacement

1 Offer up the kickstart shaft ensuring that the bearings locate on their respective dowel pins. In order to pre-tension the kickstart spring, commence by fitting the central clip which retains the complete shaft assembly in position. Slacken off the kickstart stop pin.
2 Temporarily fit the kickstart lever making sure it is adequately secured so that damage will not occur to the splines when it is operated by hand.
3 From the left hand side, rotate the kickstart lever clockwise until the end of the spring locates in its socket in the crankcase.
4 Continue turning the kickstart lever, through about 200°, until the kickstart stop plate appears above the kickstart stop pin (which was slackened).
5 Hold the lever in this position while screwing in the kickstart stop pin. Upon releasing the lever, the stop plate will engage with the stop pin and the spring is now fully tensioned.
6 It is advisable to check that the kickstart return spring is still in a serviceable condition since replacement at a later stage will necessitate a further complete engine strip. If in doubt, renew. A replacement spring is a low cost item. Check also that the oil seal has been renewed in order to prevent oil leakage from the reassembled unit.

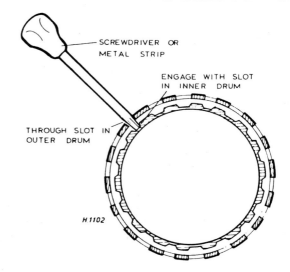

Fig. 1.5. Spragging the clutch

27 Engine and gearbox reassembly - fitting the crankshaft

1 The crankshaft assembly can be fitted to the lower crankcase immediately following reassembly of the gearbox components. The extreme right hand main bearing is located by a 'C' ring which must be positioned first; the other two main bearings have depressions in their outer faces which must register with dowel pins in the lower bearing housings.
2 Check that the oil seals are seating correctly in their housings. It may be necessary to lightly tap the crankshaft assembly in order to ensure all components are seating correctly prior to the attachment of the upper crankcase.

28 Engine and gearbox reassembly - attaching the upper crankcase

1 Before the upper crankcase is lowered into position it is first necessary to coat the mating face of the lower crankcase with a thin layer of gasket cement. No gasket is used at this joint, in consequence a perfect seal is necessary to prevent crankcase compression. Use a cement of the non-drying type, which will make any later dismantling operation much easier.
2 Lower the upper crankcase into position, making sure it registers with the two dowel pins located at the front and rear of the lower crankcase. Replace the four bolts, one of which is close to the oil pump housing, and tighten them.
3 Invert the now complete crankcase assembly and replace the sixteen bolts. A number is cast into the crankcase close to each of the bolt holes, to indicate the sequence in which they should be tightened.

29 Engine and gearbox reassembly - replacing the gear selector pawls

1 As mentioned previously, the ratchet drive for changing the gears is located in the end of the cam.
2 Replace the 'T' plate which retains the cam in position. Also replace the pawl striker plate. This plate depresses the ratchet drive when the pawls are rotated. If the sliding face is worn, renew the plate otherwise selection problems will occur.
3 Replace the 'C' plate which retains the drive shaft. All three of these plates are held in position by two crosshead screws which should be tightened with an impact screwdriver.
4 Slide the gearchange lever shaft through the engine from the right hand side - do not forget the gearchange return spring which is positioned between the quadrant and the crankcase.

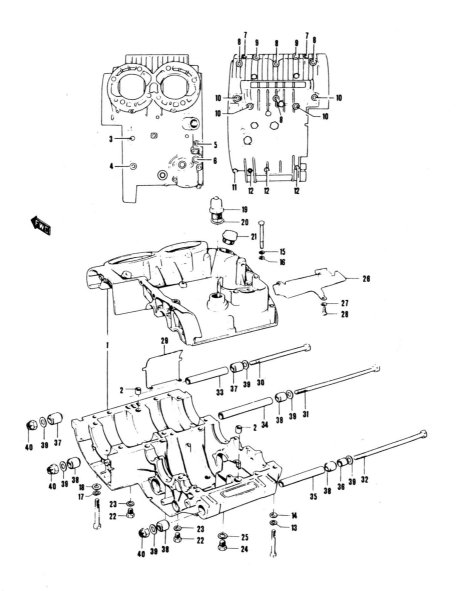

FIG. 1.6. CRANKCASES

1	Crankcase assembly	21	Oil plug
2	Dowel pin (2 off)	22	Crankcase drain plug (3 off)
3	Bolt	23	Drain plug washer (3 off)
4	Bolt	24	Gearbox drain plug
5	Bolt	25	Drain plug washer
6	Bolt	26	Oil spray plate
7	Bolt (2 off)	27	Spring washer (3 off)
8	Bolt (4 off)	28	Screw - plate mounting (3 off)
9	Bolt (2 off)	29	Oil spray plate
10	Bolt (4 off)	30	Front engine bolt
11	Bolt	31	Centre engine bolt
12	Bolt (3 off)	32	Rear engine bolt
13	Spring washer (8 off)	33	Front support bush spacer
14	Washer (8 off)	34	Centre support bush spacer
15	Spring washer (2 off)	35	Rear support bush spacer
16	Washer (2 off)	36	Spacer
17	Spring washer (10 off)	37	Flexible bush (2 off)
18	Washer (10 off)	38	Flexible bush (4 off)
19	Breather plug	39	Washer (6 off)
20	Breather plug washer	40	Nut (3 off)

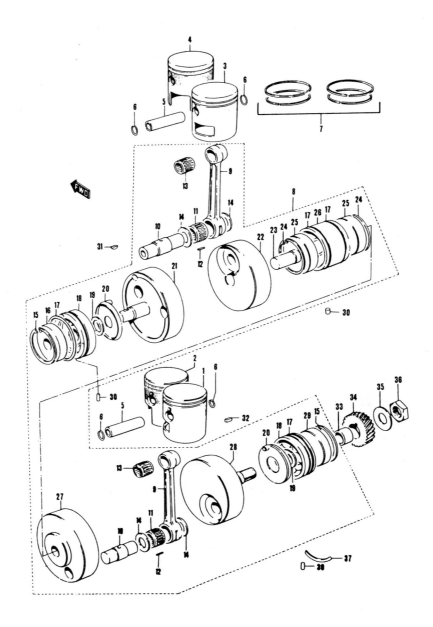

FIG. 1.7. PISTONS AND CRANKSHAFT ASSEMBLY

1	RH/LH piston alternative	20	Oil guide plate (2 off)
2	RH/LH piston alternative	21	LH crankshaft/flywheel
3	RH/LH piston alternative	22	LH central flywheel
4	RH/LH piston alternative	23	Central crankshaft
5	Gudgeon pin (2 off)	24	Circlip (2 off)
6	Gudgeon pin circlip (4 off)	25	Central oil seals (2 off)
7	Piston ring assembly	26	Central crankshaft bearing
8	Crankshaft assembly	27	RH central flywheel
9	Con rod (2 off)	28	RH crankshaft/flywheel
10	Crank pin (2 off)	29	Oil seal
11	Big end needle roller cage (2 off)	30	Dowel pin - bearing locator (3 off)
12	Big end needle roller cage (32 off)	31	Woodruff key - rotor
13	Small end bearing (2 off)	32	Woodruff key - primary pinion
14	Thrust washer (4 off)	33	Primary pinion spacer
15	Oil seal retaining circlip (2 off)	34	Primary drive pinion
16	Oil seal	35	Washer
17	'O' ring (4 off)	36	Nut
18	Crankshaft main bearings (2 off)	37	'C' ring
19	Thrust washer (2 off)		

Note that the 'flat' side of the spring is next to the quadrant; the prongs of the spring go either side of the selector rod blanking plug which also acts as the gearchange stop.
5 Temporarily fit the gearchange lever and ensure that all the gears can be selected. The engine will require turning over using the kickstart. If the engine is very stiff, strip the motor and investigate.
6 Ensure that the six tooth quadrant is centrally aligned with the FIVE tooth side of the gearchange dog.

30 Engine and gearbox reassembly - fitting the oil pump and tachometer drive

1 From the top of the crankcase, insert the oil pump drive in its mounting so that the worm engages with the worm drive on the left hand side of the kickstart pinion.
2 Refit the oil pump complete with a new gasket, ensuring that the drive flat of the shaft engages in the slot of the oil pump.
3 It is not normally necessary to remove the oil feed pipes from the crankcases. However, if this has been done, replace them at this stage, ensuring that they are scrupulously clean and that new washers are used either side of each union. Replace the nylon oil pipe cover (one screw on the right hand side and one bolt on the left hand side).
4 Do not replace the oil pump cover at this stage, since it will be necessary to gain access to the pump union bolt when the pump is bled at a later stage.

31 Engine and gearbox reassembly - refitting the primary drive and clutch

1 Slide the spacer into the oil seal on the crankshaft (right hand side).
2 Replace the engine pinion after positioning the Woodruff key in the end of the right hand crankshaft. The pinion is retained by a nut and tab washer; it must be tightened fully, with the engine locked by means of a stout rod passed through both connecting rods. Bend the tab washer to secure the nut, after the latter has been tightened.
3 Replace the outer drum of the clutch on the gearbox mainshaft. It is preceded by a thrust washer and a bush which acts as a spacer. Subsequently, replace the second thrust washer.
4 Fit the inner drum of the clutch, tab washer and securing nut. Lock the engine in position and tighten the centre nut fully before securing it with the tab washer. It will be necessary to, once again, 'sprag' the inner drum with the outer drum during the tightening operation, see Fig 1.5. Extreme care is necessary during this operation, to prevent damage to any of the castings.
5 Fit the clutch plates, commencing with a plain metal plate which engages with the serrations of the inner drum. There are seven plain and seven friction plates to be inserted alternately, ending with a friction plate.
6 Fit the clutch pushrod end piece, with the longer shouldered end within the hollow mainshaft. Do not omit the oil seal which locates with the other end of the end piece which projects from the shaft. It seats against the shoulder.
7 Fit the clutch pressure plate and then the six clutch springs together with their retaining bolts and washers. Tighten each bolt fully until it is firmly seated.

32 Engine and gearbox reassembly - fitting the right hand crankcase cover

1 The right hand side of the crankcase assembly is now complete and the end cover can be added. It is located by two dowel pins at the front and rear. A gasket is used at this joint, but there is no necessity for gasket cement unless the mating surfaces are in poor condition.
2 The cover is retained by a total of nine crosshead screws - the tenth screw is the oil level plug. Tighten these fully. Note: Allen screw conversions are available for this cover and should be used if an impact screwdriver is not available and oil seepage is a

problem. However, extreme care must always be taken when using steel screws in an aluminium casting because of the risk of stripping the threads.

33 Engine and gearbox reassembly - fitting the neutral contact and final drive sprocket

1 Reverting to the left hand side of the engine, fit the neutral gear electrical contact to the end of the gear selector drum. It is retained by a countersunk screw through the centre.
2 Fit the outer cover of the neutral contact, which is made of a plastic material and has an internal brass segment wiper contact. Make sure the contact surface is clean and free from oil.
3 The outer cover is fitted with the terminal uppermost. It has an internal O ring seal, which must be replaced if it is in any way damaged. Tighten fully the two small crosshead screws which hold the cover in position.
4 Replace the oil seal and O-ring in the gearbox drive shaft retaining plate. If there is any doubt as to the condition of these components they should be renewed. Refit the plate with the four countersunk crosshead screws. Do not forget the engine sprocket spacer.
5 Replace the final drive sprocket on the splines of the gearbox layshaft, followed by the tab washer and the centre retaining nut. Lock the engine and tighten the centre nut fully before the tab washer is bent into the locking position.

34 Engine and gearbox reassembly - refitting the alternator

1 Replace the generator rotor on the left hand end of the crankshaft, after locating the Woodruff key. A taper joint fitting is used; when the rotor is located correctly, fit also the contact breaker cam and the rotor retaining bolt with its spring washer. The contact breaker cam can be fitted in only one position, as determined by the dowel pin in its base which will engage with the keyway of the rotor.
2 Tighten the rotor bolt fully, with the engine locked in position.
3 Before the stator plate assembly is slid into position, thread the wiring harness through the aperture in the crankcase housing.
4 Fit the stator plate assembly by sliding it over the rotor. The stator plate is held by 3 long crosshead screws which screw into the crankcase. When the stator plate has been secured fully, the plate containing the grommet through which the wiring harness passes can be attached to the crankcase by its retaining crosshead screw. This will form an effective seal to the rear of the left hand crankcase cover when it is attached at a later stage.
5 Do not omit to attach the blue coloured wire to the terminal of the neutral contact cover.
6 Later, after refitting the pistons and barrels, check that the ignition timing is still correct by aligning the timing marks of the rotor with the line on the stator plate. A full explanation of checking and resetting the ignition timing is given in Chapter 3 of this manual.

35 Engine and gearbox reassembly - fitting the left hand crankcase cover

1 Before the rear left hand crankcase cover is replaced, it is necessary to insert the clutch pushrod into the hollow gearbox mainshaft.
2 Replace the spacer over the gearchange shaft. This spacer serves to protect the shaft from a slack rear chain.
3 It is advisable to check the action of the clutch operating worm, the mechanism of which is attached to the inner side of the left hand crankcase cover. The mode of operation is both simple and self-explanatory; if the operating action is harsh or uneven, the assembly should be dismantled and well greased prior to reassembly.
4 Replace both front and rear engine covers. The addition of these covers at this stage is recommended only as a temporary

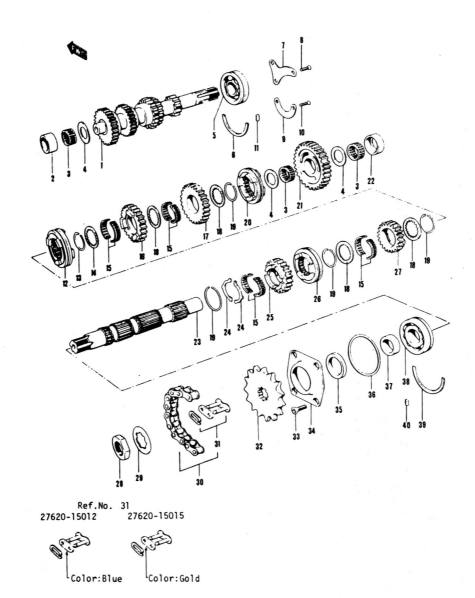

Ref.No. 31
27620-15012   27620-15015

Color:Blue   Color:Gold

FIG. 1.8. GEAR CLUSTERS

1	Mainshaft	21	1st driven gear wheel
2	Outer bush	22	Outer bush
3	Needle roller bearing (3 off)	23	Final drive shaft
4	Thrust washer (3 off)	24	5th driven gear ring (2 off)
5	Ball bearing	25	5th driven gear ring
6	'C' ring	26	5th driven gear wheel
7	Oil reservoir cap plate	27	4th driven gear
8	Screw (3 off)	28	Engine sprocket nut
9	Drive shaft bearing retaining plate	29	Tab washer
10	Screw (2 off)	30	Chain assembly
11	Dowel pin (2 off)	31	Spring link
12	3rd driven gear wheel	32	Engine sprocket
13	Circlip	33	Screw (4 off)
14	Washer	34	Drive shaft oil seal plate
15	Driven gear bearing set (4 off)	35	Drive shaft oil seal plate
16	3rd driven gear	36	'O' ring
17	2nd driven gear	37	Engine sprocket spacer
18	Washer (4 off)	38	Ball bearing
19	Circlip (4 off)	39	'C' ring
20	1st driven gear wheel	40	Dowel pin (2 off)

expedient to prevent damage to the alternator and also to protect hands from the sprocket whilst the engine is being refitted. They will have to be detached later to insert the clutch cable and check the timing.

5 Re-attach the alternator cable loom to the top of the crankcase.

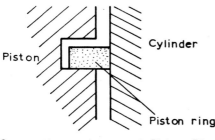

Conventional piston and Piston Ring

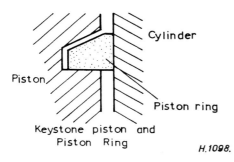

Keystone piston and Piston Ring   H.1098.

Fig. 1.9. Ring profiles

36 Engine and gearbox reassembly - refitting the pistons and cylinder barrels

1 Before commencing assembly of the pistons and cylinder barrels, pad the mouth of each crankcase with clean rag, to prevent any misplaced component from dropping in. Replace the needle roller bearings in the connecting rod eyes.

2 Fit each piston in turn, complete with rings. If the gudgeon pins are a tight fit in the piston bosses, warm the pistons first by placing a rag soaked in hot water on the crown.

3 Use only new circlips and make sure each is positively located after the gudgeon pins have been pressed home. Never be tempted to re-use the original circlips; if they work loose as a result of having lost their tension, serious engine damage is inevitable.

4 Make sure both small ends are well lubricated by using a hand oil can filled with engine oil. Pump some into the crankshaft and big end assemblies too, before the cylinder barrels are fitted. This will necessitate removing the rag which pads each crankcase, which should be replaced until the pistons and piston rings have engaged with each cylinder bore.

5 Before refitting each cylinder barrel, oil the bore surfaces. If the cylinders have been rebored, check to ensure the edges of the ports have been rounded off correctly. Details are given in Section 19.8 of this Chapter. Fit new base gaskets (no cement).

6 Before inserting each piston into its respective cylinder barrel, check that the piston rings are aligned correctly with regard to their end pegs. Failure to observe this precaution will lead to ring breakages, apart from extreme difficulty in fitting.

7 The pistons should be replaced in their original order, as defined by the marks scratched on the inside of the skirt during the dismantling operation. Make sure that the arrow stamped on the crown of each piston faces the forward direction ie the front of the machine.

8 There is a generous taper on the base of each cylinder barrel which should act as a good lead-in and obviate the need for a

piston ring compressor. Feed each ring into the cylinder bore separately, using as little force as possible. When the pistons and rings are well up the cylinder bores, remove the rag padding from the crankcase mouths and lower the cylinder barrels until they seat firmly on their base gaskets.

9 Holding down the cylinder barrels by hand, rotate the engine a few times in both directions to make quite sure both pistons are running free in the bores. If everything appears in order, the cylinder heads can be fitted.

37 Engine and gearbox reassembly - refitting the cylinder heads

1 Place a new aluminium cylinder head gasket on each cylinder barrel.

2 Fit the cylinder head bolts and tighten them down until they begin to bite. Then tighten each cylinder head separately, in a diagonal sequence, tightening each bolt a little at a time. Continue tightening in the diagonal sequence until the recommended torque wrench setting is obtained.

3 Refit the spark plugs, if only as a temporary expedient, to prevent foreign matter from dropping into the engine whilst it is being replaced. Do not over-tighten; it is sufficient to obtain a good seating between the plugs, their sealing washers and the cylinder heads, without excessive force.

38 Engine and gearbox reassembly - refitting the twin carburettors

1 Place new gaskets over each set of carburettor mounting studs and replace the two inlet manifolds.

2 Replace the carburettors and tighten the clips around the manifolds.

3 Join together both chokes by means of the common operating rod, which is retained by a split pin through the extreme right hand end.

39 Replacing the engine and gearbox unit in the frame

1 This is a task requiring the assistance of a second person because the complete engine unit is heavy and needs to be supported whilst the engine bolts are replaced.

2 Lift the complete unit into the frame and lower it in approximately the correct position until it rests on the lower frame tubes. It is probably easier if the engine is lifted in from the left, where there should be adequate access.

3 The engine bolts are all of the same diameter but have different lengths. The short bolt locates at the front of the engine and the longest bolt goes underneath. The remaining bolt supports the rear of the engine. It is customary to fit the engine bolts from the left hand side of the machine, using a second person to feed them into position whilst the engine unit is lifted.

4 Support the engine unit and lift it slightly in the frame until the engine mounting lugs correspond with the engine bolt holes in the frame. Locate the rearmost engine bolt first, noting that it has a spacer close to the left hand rear mounting plate. Fit the front engine bolt next, then the engine bolt which fits below the engine.

5 Each engine bolt has a nut, of the self-locking type, and a washer. Tighten all three bolts fully to obviate the risk of engine vibration.

6 When the engine is firmly secured, remove the final drive sprocket cover and refit the final drive chain by positioning both ends in the teeth of the rear wheel sprocket and add the spring link. Make sure the spring clip is located positively, with the closed end facing the direction of travel. Adjust the chain to the correct tension, by following the procedure described in Chapter 5.

7 Refit the chainguard.

8 Screw the clutch cable adjuster into the final drive cover as far as it will go. Replace the clutch operating mechanism (two crosshead screws) and attach the small return spring. Attach the

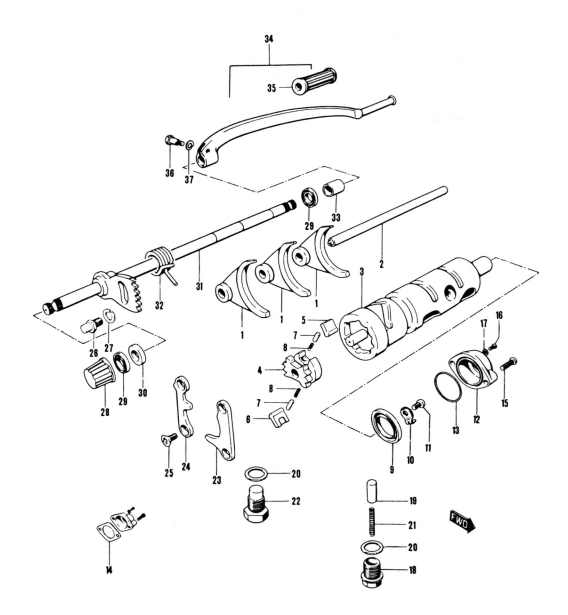

FIG. 1.10. GEAR CHANGE MECHANISM

1	Selector fork (3 off)	20	Plug washer (2 off)
2	Selector fork shaft	21	Spring
3	Gear change cam	22	Gearchange cam guide bolt
4	Cam operating gear	23	Gearchange striker plate
5	Gear change pawl	24	Cam retainer
6	Gear change pawl	25	Screw (4 off)
7	Ratchet plunger (2 off)	26	Selector shaft blank/gearchange stop
8	Plunger spring (2 off)	27	Spring washer
9	Cam oil seal	28	Gearchange shaft plastic cap
10	Neutral switch contact	29	Gearchange shaft oil seal (2 off)
11	Screw	30	Cushion pad
12	Neutral switch/cover	31	Gearchange shaft
13	'O' ring	32	Gearchange shaft return spring
14	Switch gasket (T500 only)	33	Spacer
15	Screw (2 off)	34	Gearchange lever
16	Electrical screw	35	Gearchange lever rubber
17	Washer	36	Bolt
18	Gearchange cam stop plug	37	Spring washer
19	Plunger		

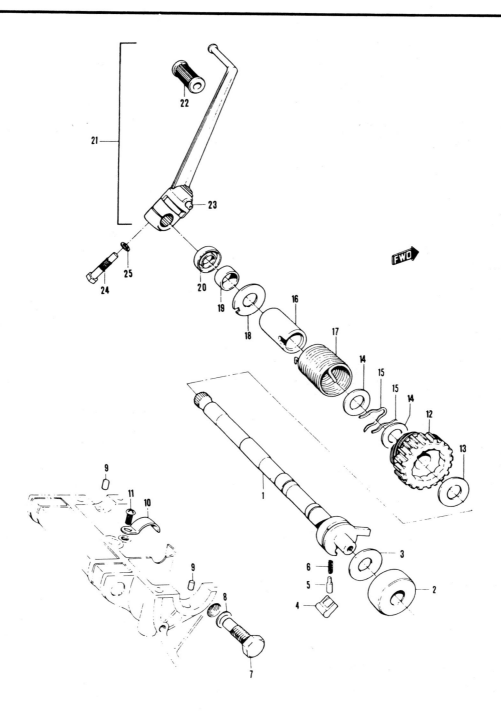

FIG. 1.11. KICKSTART ASSEMBLY

1	Kickstarter shaft	14	Thrust washer (2 off)
2	RH bush	15	Circlip (2 off)
3	Thrust washer	16	Kickstart return spring inner guide
4	Kickstart pawl	17	Kickstart return spring inner guide
5	Pawl plunger	18	Washer
6	Plunger spring	19	LH bush
7	Kickstart stop bolt	20	Oil seal
8	Washer	21	Kickstart lever assembly
9	Dowel pin (2 off)	22	Kickstart lever rubber
10	Clamp - shaft	23	Grease nipple
11	Screw	24	Kickstart lever pinch bolt
12	Kickstart - drive gear	25	Spring washer
13	Thrust washer		

25.2 Slide the gearchange cam into position

25.3 Left to right: Gearchange cam stop, gearchange cam guide and gearbox oil drain plug

25.4 Showing the selector forks located on the fork rod and the pegs aligned with the holes in the cam

25.5a Replace the 'C' rings for the location of the mainshaft ...

25.5b ... and final drive shaft bearings

25.6 Replace the drive shaft ensuring the gear wheels locate with the fork ends

25.7a Locate the rear oil splash plate and ...

25.7b ... replace the mainshaft

26.1a Fit the central clip and crosshead screw which retains the kickstart shaft

26.1b Slacken off the kickstart stop pin

28.2 Lower the upper crankcase into position, locating on the two dowel pins

28.3 The lower crankcase showing the sixteen crankcase bolts, three crankcase drain bolts, gearbox drain plug and the two gearchange cam locating bolts

29.3 Replace the drive shaft plate, cam retaining plate and striker plate

29.6 Ensure that the six tooth quadrant is centrally aligned with the five tooth gearchange dog

30.1 Showing the position of the oil pump drive shaft — upper crankcase removed

31.1 Replace the crankshaft spacer and Woodruff key

31.2 Drive pinion onto crankshaft until it seats against the spacer

31.3a Slide the first thrust washer and spacer/bush on the gearbox mainshaft

31;3b Replace the outer drum

31.3c Do not forget the second thrust washer

31.4 Replace the clutch inner drum

31.5a Fit the clutch plates, commencing with a plain metal plate...

31.5b ... and alternating with friction plates

31.6 Insert the clutch pushrod end piece

31.7 Fit the clutch pressure plate, springs and bolts and washers

32.1 Refitting the engine cover with a new gasket. Note locating dowels

33.1 Replace the countersunk screw and contact in the gear-change cam

33.4 Driveshaft retaining plate and new oil seal

33.5 Final drive sprocket, nut and tab washer

34.1a Replace the Woodruffe key followed by the rotor ...

34.1b ... contact breaker cam, bolt and spring washer

34.4 Thread cable through aperture in crankcase and mount stator plate

35.1 Don't forget to insert the clutch pushrod after replacing the mainshaft seal

35.2 Replace the spacer over the gearchange shaft

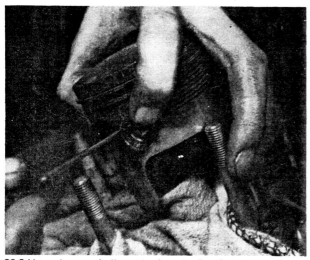

36.3 Use only new circlips at both ends of each gudgeon pin

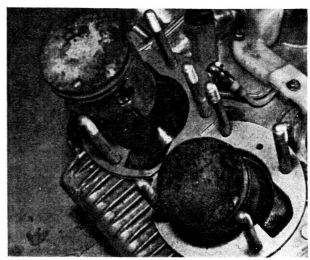

36.5 Fit new cylinder base gaskets

36.8 Ease the cylinders over the pistons individually

37.1 Use only new cylinder head gaskets

37.2 Note the plain and spring washer under each cylinder head nut and bolt

39.3 The rear engine bolt has a spacer between the frame and the engine unit

39.6 Refit the spring link with the closed end of link facing the direction of travel

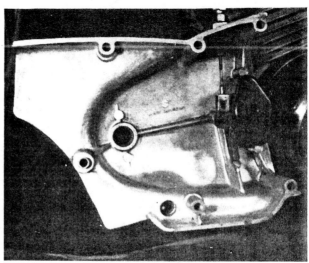

39.7 The final drive cover contains the clutch cable, operating mechanism and retaining spring

clutch cable to the operating arm and also to the handlebar lever. Refit the cover with the six crosshead screws. There is no need for a gasket or gasket cement.

9 Refit the kickstart and gearchange pedal. Set the timing and replace the alternator cover.

10 Replace both carburettor tops, with their respective slide and needle assemblies. Care is necessary to ensure the needles engage with the needle jet orifice and the slides with their grooves in line with the pegs in the carburettor body. Check that both slides operate correctly as the throttle is opened and closed; it is easy for a throttle cable to become displaced during the fitting operation.

11 Refit the air cleaner box complete. This is held to the frame by two crosshead screws and their nuts through lugs at the front and rear. Slide the air hoses over the carburettor intakes and secure them in position with their respective clips.

12 Replace the battery and reconnect the electrical leads both to the battery and from the generator wiring harness and snap connectors. Colour coding eliminates the possibility of cross-connection. The battery is retained by a strap and seats on a moulded rubber mat. Make sure the overflow pipe is connected; it is led away via a small bracket attached to the rear subframe so that battery acid will not damage the paintwork.

13 Replace the cover which fits over the battery housing and the electrical connections. This fits over two lugs attached to the seat tube and is held in position by a captive screwed knob. This cover contains also the tool roll, which is retained behind a flat spring clamp.

14 Replace both footrests. Note how an extension of each footrest has a separate bolt fixing to the frame, to prevent the footrests from rotating. The right hand footrest holds the brake pedal in position. Reconnect the rear brake return spring.

15 Reconnect the rear brake operating cable to the brake pedal. Make sure the clevis pin is greased and a new split pin is used to retain the clevis pin in position.

16 Connect the stop lamp switch operating arm to the brake pedal by means of the spring connection. The end of the spring threads through the small hole in the top of the brake pedal arm. Check whether both the brake and the stop lamp are operating correctly and adjust either or both as necessary. The stop lamp switch has a threaded body permitting it to be either raised or lowered. The lower the switch, the later its action and vice-versa.

40 Reconnecting the oil pump control cable and oil pump feed

1 Returning to the right hand side of the machine, screw the oil pump cable adjuster into its support projecting from the crankcase. Fit the small barrel-shaped nipple over the fixing on the end of the control cable and insert this in the spring-loaded operating arm of the oil pump. The control cable is a take-off from the throttle cable junction box and passes through a cable adjuster and guide fitted close to the oil pump. A rubber sleeve fits over the cable and the adjuster, to exclude water.

2 Pump adjustment is correct when the line inscribed on the operating arm is aligned exactly with the line inscribed on the oil pump body, when the throttle is fully open. If adjustment is necessary, the cable adjuster can be used to either increase or decrease the operating arm movement. Check also that a second line inscribed on the operating arm corresponds when the throttle is closed.

3 Remove the 6 mm bolt which acts as a temporary plug to the oil feed union and reconnect the oil feed pipe which is attached to the pump. Fit new washers to the banjo union, to obviate the risk of oil leakage in service.

4 Bleed the feed pipe to the oil pump by slackening the large union nut at the forward end of the oil pump. Oil should be drained off from this point until the feed pipe is entirely free of air bubbles. If the oil does not flow out of the bleed valve, prime the pump by opening the throttle fully and turning the engine over with the kickstart until the inlet system is bled. Retighten the union nut and drain the crankcases of fuel if necessary. In addition, if the oil feeds from the pump have been removed from

39.9 Replace the carburettor tops complete with needles, springs, slides and cables

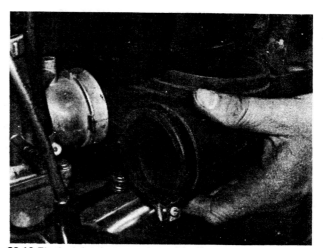

39.10 Fit the inlet duct complete with clips

39.11a Replace the battery mat and battery and re-connect the leads

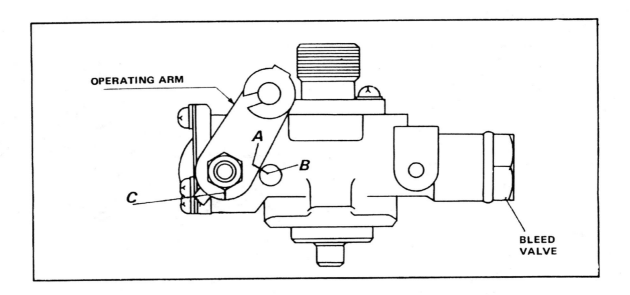

Fig. 1.12. Oil pump

For correct operation:—
A and B should align with the throttle open. Check that C and B also align for throttle fully closed.

the crankcase, they will also require bleeding. Inject engine oil into all the union holes in the crankcase and pour some oil into each oil pipe. Connect the pipes in position and proceed to Section 42.7, carrying out all the intermediate steps except for fitting the oil pump cover.

5   Refit the oil pump cover and reconnect the tachometer drive.

41 Refitting the exhaust pipes and silencers

1   Before refitting the exhaust system, check that the exhaust system is clean, particularly the detachable baffles fitted to the silencers. A two-stroke engine is particularly susceptible to back pressure caused by blocked or partially blocked exhaust systems, due to the oily nature of the exhaust gases and the resultant build up of sludge.

2   Do not be tempted to replace the exhaust system without the baffles in the silencers because this will have a very adverse effect on performance. The greatly increased exhaust note may give the illusion of more speed; it is entirely false. Engine damage is liable to occur if the machine is run in this condition for an extended period.

3   When the exhaust pipes are fitted to the cylinder barrels, use new sealing washers at the port joint. Replace the exhaust systems and clamps and secure in position with the bolts - two off per clamp.

4   The silencers are held to their respective frame number by the pillion footrests, which pass through lugs welded to the top of each silencer body. The silencers have an extra bracket to which is attached a rubber stop to cushion the centre stand when it is retracted.

5   Check that the screw retaining each baffle tube in the silencer ends is tight. If the screw works loose, it will eventually fall out and the baffle tubes will work free.

42 Starting and running the rebuilt engine

1   Add the correct amount of SAE 10W/40 motor oil to the gearbox. T500 models require 1400 cc of oil and GT500A models require 1600 cc of oil. It is essential to add a measured amount rather than rely upon the gearbox level plug because the quantity of oil was increased in light of service experience, and the correct level would be well above that of the original level plug hole.

2   Adjust the clutch by, initially, unscrewing the locknut in the centre of the clutch operating mechanism. Insert a screwdriver and turn the rod either in or out until the screw just touches the pushrod through the middle of the gearbox layshaft. Screw back ¼ of a turn and lock in position. Using the cable adjusters, remove the slack from the cable until there is 4 mm (0.16 inch) free movement at the handlebar lever. Check the operation of the clutch and replace the blanking cover.

3   Check that the throttle cables are properly adjusted using the adjuster at the handlebar end.

4   Tension the rear chain and check the operation of the front and rear brakes.

5   Replace the plug caps. Connect the petrol feed pipes to the carburettors and also the pipe from the flange of the left hand carburettor to the diaphragm chamber of the petrol tap. This latter pipe is reinforced by an outer coil spring. All pipes have push-on connections.

6   Set the tap in the 'Prime' position, close the chokes and switch on the ignition. After a few depressions of the kickstarter, the engine should fire and commence to run. Raise the chokes as soon as possible, without causing the engine to stall.

7   With the engine running at between 1500 and 2000 rpm open the oil pump fully by pulling on the operating cable. Continue running with the oil pump in this position until all oil bubbles are expelled from the oil pipes attached to the upper crankcase. Stop the engine and return the control cable to its normal operating position, making sure the cable end is not displaced from the guide. It will be appreciated that the machine will smoke excessively whilst the engine is run with the oil pump

open fully, but this is the only effective way to bleed air from the feed pipes. Excess oil may be drained from the crankcases after the engine has stopped, by removing the 14 mm drain plugs. Replace the cover over the crankcase oil pipes, check the marks on the oil pump and ensure the level of oil in the oil tank is well above the sight glass minimum level. Temporarily disconnect the tachometer drive to fit the oil pump cover (early models only).

8 Check the exterior of the engine for signs of oil leaks or blowing gaskets. Before taking the machine on the road for the first time, check that all nuts and bolts are tight and nothing has been omitted during the reassembly sequence.

43 Taking the rebuilt machine on the road

1 Any rebuilt engine will take time to settle down, even if parts have been replaced in their original order. For this reason it is highly advisable to treat the machine gently for the first few miles, so that oil can circulate properly and the new parts have a reasonable chance to bed down.

2 Even greater care is necessary if the engine has been rebored or if a new crankshaft has been fitted. In the case of a rebore, the engine will have to be run-in again as if the machine were new. This means more use of the gearbox and a restraining hand on the throttle until at least 500 miles have been covered. There is no point in keeping to any set speed limit; the main need is to keep only a light load on the engine and to gradually work up the performance until the 500 mile mark is reached. As a general guide, it is inadvisable to exceed 4000 rpm during the first 500 miles and 5000 rpm for the next 500 miles. These periods can be lessened when a new crankshaft only is fitted; experience is the best guide since it is easy to tell when the engine will run freely.

3 If at any time the oil feed shows signs of failure, stop the engine immediately and investigate the cause. If the engine is run without oil, even for a short period, irreparable engine damage is inevitable.

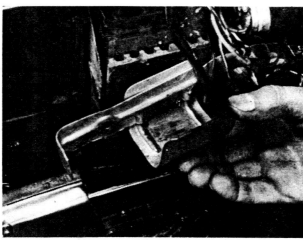

39.11b Fit the battery strap/tool holder

39.15 Do not omit split pin through end of brake pedal clevis pin

40.1 Screw oil pump cable into its support and affix the detachable nipple

41.3 Use only new sealing washers at the exhaust port joint

42.1 Refill the gearbox with oil

44 Fault diagnosis - engine

Symptom	Reason/s	Remedy
Engine will not start	Defective spark plugs	Remove plugs and lay on cylinder heads. Check whether spark occurs when engine is kicked over.
	Dirty or closed contact breaker points	Check condition of points and whether gap is correct.
	Air leak at crankcase or worn crankshaft oil seals	Check whether petrol is reaching the spark plugs (tap in prime position).
Engine runs unevenly	Ignition and/or fuel system fault	Check systems independently as though engine will not start.
	Blowing cylinder head gaskets	Leak should be evident from oil leakage where gas escapes.
	Incorrect ignition timing	Check timing very accurately and reset if necessary.
Lack of power	Fault in fuel system or incorrect ignition timing	See above.
	Choked silencers	Remove and clean out baffles.
High fuel/oil consumption	Cylinder barrels in need of rebore and oversize pistons	Fit new rings and pistons after rebore.
	Oil leaks or air leaks from damaged gaskets or oil seals	Trace source of leak and replace damaged gasket and/or seal.
Excessive mechanical noise	Worn cylinder barrels (piston slap)	Rebore and fit oversize pistons.
	Worn small end bearings (rattle)	Replace needle roller bearings (caged) and if necessary, gudgeon pins.
	Worn big end bearings (knock)	Fit replacement crankshaft assembly.
	Worn main bearings (rumble)	Fit new journal bearings and seals. If centre bearing, new crankshaft.
Engine overheats and fades	Pre-ignition and/or weak mixture	Check carburettor settings. Check whether plug grades correct.
	Lubrication failure	Check oil pump setting and whether oil tank is empty.

45 Fault diagnosis - clutch

Symptom	Reason/s	Remedy
Engine speed increases as shown by	Clutch slip	Check clutch adjustment for free play at

tachometer but machine does not respond

Symptom	Reason/s	Remedy
		handlebar lever. Check condition of clutch plate linings, also whether clutch spring bolts are tight.
Difficulty in engaging gears. Gear changes jerky and machine creeps forward, even when clutch is withdrawn. Difficulty in selecting neutral	Clutch drag	Check clutch adjustment for too much free play. Check for burrs on clutch plate tongues or indentations in clutch drum slots. Dress with file if damage not too great. Check for warpage of clutch plates. Check grade of oil used.
	Clutch assembly loose on mainshaft	Check tightness of retaining nut. If loose, fit new tab washer and retighten.
Operation action stiff	Damaged, trapped or frayed control cable	Check cable and replace if necessary. Make sure cable is lubricated and has no sharp bends.
	Bent pushrods	Replace.

46 Fault diagnosis - gearbox

Symptom	Reason/s	Remedy
Difficulty in engaging gears	Gear selector forks bent	Replace.
	Gear clusters assembled incorrectly	Check that thrust washers are located correctly.
	Gear selector forks worn	Replace.
Machine jumps out of gear	Worn dogs on ends of gear pinions	Replace pinions involved.
	Cam plate pawls stuck	Free pawl assembly.
Gear lever does not return to normal position	Broken return spring	Replace spring.
Kickstart does not return when engine is turned over or started	Broken or poorly tensioned return spring	Replace spring or re-tension.
Kickstart slips	Kickstart drive pinion internals, pawls or springs worn badly	Replace all worn parts.

Chapter 2 Fuel System and Lubrication

Contents

Specifications

Fuel tank capacity

All models ... ...   3.1 Imp gallons (3.7 US gallons/14 litres)
    3.7 Imp gallons (4.5 US gallons/17 litres)

Oil tank capacity

All models ... ...   3.16 pints (3.80 US pints/1.8 litres)

Carburettors

	T500	T500II	T500III	T500R	T500J	T500K	T500L	GT500A
Make				Mikuni				
Type	VM34SC			VM 32 SC				
Main jet	410			150		97.5		97.5
Slow running jet	25			30				30
Needle	5DP2			SEP8		5FP17-3		5FP17-3
Throttle valve				2.5				2.5

1 General description

The fuel system comprises a petrol tank from which petrol is fed by gravity to the twin carburettors, via a petrol tap of the diaphragm type. The tap is of unusual construction in the sense that it has no 'off' position. The flow of petrol is controlled by a diaphragm, which is actuated by vacuum from the left hand carburettor flange. During each inlet cycle, the diaphragm is deflected by the vacuum effect, permitting petrol to flow to the two float chambers. When the engine stops, the diaphragm returns to its original position and the flow of petrol is shut off.

All models are fitted with twin carburettors of Mikuni manufacture which have integral float chambers and manually-operated chokes. The administration of the correct petrol/air mixture to the engine is controlled by a conventional throttle slide and needle arrangement. A large capacity air cleaner serves the dual purpose of supplying clean air to the carburettor intakes and effectively silencing the intake 'roar'.

Unlike most two-strokes of conventional design, the Suzuki twins do not depend on a petrol/oil mix for engine lubrication.

They utilise the 'Posi-Force' (or 'CCI') lubrication system which takes the form of a separate oil supply contained in an oil tank which is fed by gravity to an oil pump interconnected with the throttle. The oil pump provides a pressure feed to the crankshaft, big ends and main bearings, also to the rear of each cylinder bore. The feed rate varies according to the degree of throttle opening, in a manner reminiscent of that pioneered by a British manufacturer of two-strokes during the early 1930's.

2 Petrol tank - removal and replacement

1 It is unlikely that the petrol tank will need to be removed except on very infrequent occasions, because it does not restrict access to the engine unless a top overhaul is to be carried out whilst the engine is in the frame.

2 The petrol tank is secured at the rear by a single bolt, washer and rubber buffer that threads into a strut welded across the two top frame tubes. It is necessary first to remove the dual seat before access is available.

3 When the bolt and washer are withdrawn, the petrol tank can be lifted clear from the frame. The nose of the tank is a push fit over two small rubber buffers, attached to a peg that projects from each side of the frame, immediately to the rear of the steering head. A small rubber 'mat' cushions the rear of the tank and prevents contact with the two top frame tubes.
4 Early models have a 'screw down' type filler cap on the petrol tank; later models utilise a quick action, flip-up type.
5 Unlike most two-strokes, there is no dependence on the use of a petrol/oil mix for lubrication of the engine. The engine lubrication system is quite separate and in consequence only petrol alone is carried in the petrol tank.

2.2 The petrol tank is secured at the rear of the tank by a single bolt, washer and rubber buffer

3 Petrol tap - removal, dismantling and replacement

1 As explained earlier, the petrol tap is of the diaphragm type and has no 'off' position. It is threaded into the bottom of the petrol tank on the left hand side and has three operating positions - prime, on and reserve. The 'prime' position is for starting only. Do not allow the petrol tap to stay in this position for longer than one minute as it is possible to fill the crankcase with petrol, should the float stick down. The resulting hydrostatic lock can cause extensive damage to the engine. Also, the tap is designed such that, in the 'on' position no fuel will flow when the engine is stopped in order to guard against fire risks in the event of a 'tumble' or should the bike fall over.
2 Before the petrol tap can be removed, it is first necessary to drain the petrol tank. This is accomplished by turning the tap lever into the 'prime' position, when petrol will commence to flow through the tap without the engine running.
3 When the tank has been drained, unscrew the tap from the bottom of the petrol tank, using a set spanner across the flats closest to the bottom of the tank. It will be necessary to detach the three push-on pipes, one to the left hand carburettor intake flange and one each to the carburettor float chambers, before the tap is unscrewed.
4 The filter bowl is located at the base of the tap. It is retained in position by a centre bolt which should be removed to release the filter bowl, sealing gasket and filter gauze.
5 It is not recommended that the vacuum chamber is dismantled. If the unit malfunctions, a replacement tap is required.
6 The petrol tap lever assembly is held to the tap body by two small screws. It is inadvisable to disturb this assembly unless leakage occurs, in which case the sealing gaskets will have to be renewed.
7 Reassemble by reversing the dismantling procedure and check that the filter gauze is clean before the filter bowl assembly is replaced at the base of the tap. It is a wise precaution to renew

the sealing washer which may otherwise tend to leak after it has been disturbed.
8 Check also that the feed pipes and the vacuum pipe from the left hand carburettor flange are good push-on fits, secured by their respective wire clips. The condition of the vacuum pipe is of particular importance since air leaks will seriously affect the operation of the diaphragm and the carburation of the left hand cylinder. If in doubt, renew this pipe as a precaution; it is protected by an external coil spring throughout its length to prevent accidental damage and to provide additional reinforcement.

4 Carburettors - general description

1 The Mikuni twin carburettors fitted to the Suzuki 500 cc twins are of the 'homo-pressure' Amal type. A conventional throttle slide and needle arrangement is coupled with a main jet to control the amount of petrol/air mixture administered to the engine; the main jet flow is also controlled by the pressure drop in the air stream as it passes through the venturi, or bell mouth section, at the carburettor inlet. The carburettors are of identical specification, apart from the addition of a short tube to the upper portion of the left hand carburettor flange, to which the vacuum pipe for the diaphragm petrol tap is attached.
2 Air is drawn into the carburettor bell mouths via a large capacity air cleaner which has a detachable paper element. The air cleaner acts also as an effective carburettor intake silencer and eliminates induction 'roar'. The engine must not be run without the air cleaner attached because the carburettors are jetted to compensate for the slight restriction in air flow. Removal of the air cleaner will result in a greatly weakened mixture, which will cause overheating and subsequent engine damage.
3 The Mikuni VM 32 SC carburettors have been continually modified as the Suzuki T500 range of motor cycles has evolved. Although the main body of the carburettor has remained basically common, the float chamber, float and mixing chamber cap have all been modified. It is suggested that the following procedures, which apply to the latest version of the carburettor, are closely adhered to, noting any small differences which may occur.
4 A wide range of optional main jets are available if required. However, there are three distinct ranges of main jet size with a corresponding size of needle and needle jet for each range. Check the carburettor for the required range before buying alternative jets. The range is dependent on the model; see Specifications.

5 Carburettors - removal

1 Remove both carburettors either as a pair or separately by following the procedure described in Chapter 1, Section 7. They are linked together by the common choke-operated rod, which is freed by withdrawing the split pin through the extreme right hand end.
2 Check the condition of the rubber inlet manifolds and replace if they show any signs of splitting or perishing.

6 Carburettors - dismantling and reassembly

1 Invert each carburettor and remove the float chamber by withdrawing the four retaining screws. The float chamber bowls will lift away, exposing the float assembly, hinge and float needle. There is a gasket between the float chamber bowl and the carburettor body which need not be disturbed unless it is leaking.
2 With a pair of thin nosed pliers, withdraw the pin which acts as the hinge for the twin floats. This will free the floats and the float needle. Check that none of the floats has punctured and that the float needle and seating are both clean and in good condition. If the needle has a ridge, it should be renewed in

48

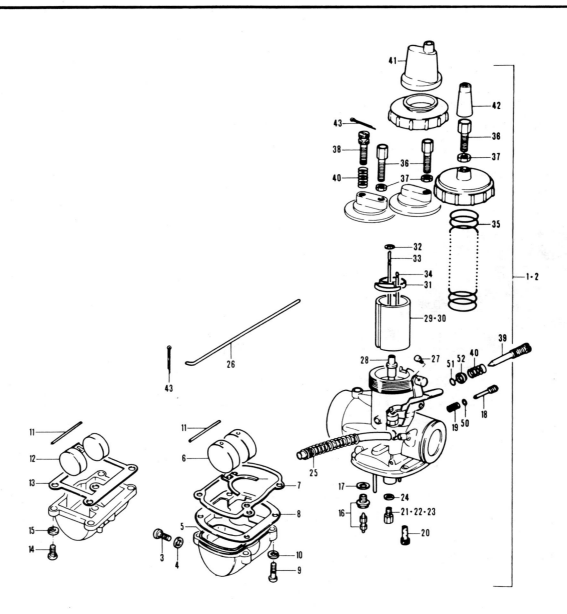

FIG. 2.1. CARBURETTOR COMPONENTS

1	RH carburettor assembly
2	LH carburettor assembly
3	Drain plug
4	Drain plug washer
5	Float chamber gasket *
6	Float * (2 off)
7	Float chamber gasket *
8	Plate *
9	Screw * (4 off)
10	Spring washer * (4 off)
11	Float pin
12	Float assembly
13	Float chamber gasket
14	Screw (4 off)
15	Spring washer (4 off)
* T500 only
16	Float needle valve assembly
17	Needle valve gasket
18	Pilot air adjusting screw
19	Pilot screw spring
20	Pilot jet
21	Main jet
22	Main jet

23	Main jet
24	Main jet washer
25	Vacuum pipe (to petrol tap)
26	Choke connecting rod
27	Choke rod bolt
28	Needle jet
29	RH throttle valve
30	LH throttle valve
31	Throttle valve spring seat
32	Needle retaining clip
33	Throttle needle
34	Throttle valve adjusting rod
35	Throttle valve spring alternatives
36	Cable adjuster
37	Cable adjuster nut
38	Throttle stop screw alternative
39	Throttle stop screw alternative
40	Throttle stop spring
41	Cable adjuster boot alternative
42	Cable adjuster boot alternative
43	Split pin

conjunction with its seating.

3 Punctured floats made of brass can be repaired by soldering, after the internal petrol has been allowed to evaporate. It is questionable whether such a repair can be justified, however, other than in an emergency because the solder will add weight to the float and thus affect the petrol level. It is generally advisable to fit a new replacement float assembly in view of the comparatively low cost involved.

4 The main jet is located in the centre of the circular mixing chamber housing. It is threaded into the base of the needle jet and can be unscrewed from the bottom of the carburettor. The needle jet lifts out from the top of the carburettor, after the main jet has been unscrewed.

5 The float needle seating is also found in the underside of the carburettor, towards the bell mouth intake. It is threaded into the carburettor body and has a fibre sealing washer fitted on the underside. If the float needle and the seating are worn, they should both be replaced, never separately. Wear usually takes the form of a ridge or groove, which may cause the needle to seat imperfectly.

6 The carburettor slides, return springs and needle assemblies, together with the mixing chamber tops, are attached to the throttle cable. The throttle cable divides into two at a junction box located within the two top frame tubes. There is also a third cable, which is used to link the oil pump with the throttle.

7 After an extended period of service the throttle slides will wear and may produce a clicking sound within each carburettor body. Wear will be evident from inspection, usually at the base of the slide and in the locating groove. Worn slides should be replaced as soon as possible because they will give rise to air leaks which will upset the carburation.

8 The needles are suspended from the slides, where they are retained by a circlip. The needle is normally suspended from the centre groove, but other grooves are provided as a means of adjustment so that the mixture strength can be either increased or decreased by raising or lowering the needle. Care is necessary when replacing the carburettor tops because the needles are easily bent if they do not locate with the needle jets.

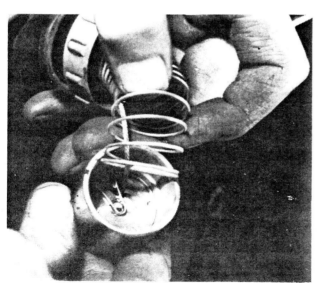

6.6 Throttle cable locates with slot in slide

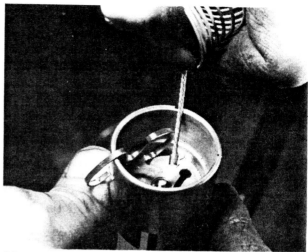

6.8 Retainer clip must be released to free cable from slide

9 The chokes are manually operated using the single lever on the left hand side of the carburettors. This cold starting system should be checked for play in the linkages as excessive wear will inhibit the required richening of the mixture. Also check that the plunger in the carburettor body is seating properly or a too rich mixture will result during normal running. When the starting (or choke) lever is depressed, it raises the starting plungers in the carburettor bodies. This allows a very rich mixture of fuel, aerated by air from the float chamber, to be mixed with air drawn through the starter air inlet (a passageway running through the carburettor body). The resultant mixture, still very rich in fuel, emerges from the starter outlet on the engine side of the throttle valve and is drawn into the engine. The accompanying component diagram shows the location of the various choke system components and their relationship with the other carburettor components.

10 Before the carburettors are reassembled, using the reversed dismantling procedure, each should be cleaned out thoroughly, preferably by the use of compressed air. Avoid using a rag because there is always risk of fine particles of lint obstructing the internal air passages or the jet orifices.

11 Never use a piece of wire or any sharp metal object to clear a blocked jet. It is only too easy to enlarge the jet under these circumstances and increase the rate of petrol consumption. Always use compressed air to clear a blockage; a tyre pump makes an admirable substitute when a compressed air line is not available.

12 Do not use excessive force when reassembling the carburettors because it is quite easy to shear the small jets or some of the smaller screws. Before attaching the air cleaner hoses, check that both throttle slides rise when the throttle is opened.

7 Carburettors - adjustment

1 When adjustments are required it is best to regard each carburettor as a separate entity. Remove the spark plug from the cylinder which is not receiving attention so that only the one cylinder will fire during the adjustments. Then change over and follow a similar routine. These adjustments should be made with the engine warm.

2 Commence operations by checking the float level, which will involve detaching the carburettor concerned, inverting it and removing the float chamber bowl. If the float level is correct the distance between the uppermost portion of the floats and the flange of the mixing chamber body will be 27.3 mm for the VM 32 SC carburettors. Adjustments are made by bending the tang on the float arm in the direction required (see accompanying diagram). Also, before replacing the float bowl, check that the

float needle is seating properly. This is accomplished by holding the carburettor body vertical with the float in the closed position and filling the fuel pipe with petrol.

3 Replace the carburettor and turn the slow running screw until it is closed fully. Then turn it back approximately 1¼ turns. Adjust the amount of play in the throttle cable to within 0.5 - 1 mm and then start the engine.

4 Slowly screw the throttle valve in and out ½ a turn (ie through one complete turn) and finally set in the position of lowest engine rpm. Re-adjust the slow running screw (pilot air screw) through a further ¼ turn and set in the position of the lowest engine rpm at which the engine runs smoothly. Note that a two-stroke engine will never fire evenly at very low engine speeds, so the setting will take the form of the best compromise. Also, if the carburettor is being set up after a complete stripdown, it may be necessary to repeat the throttle valve and pilot screw adjustments 2 or 3 times in order to obtain the best slow running characteristics.

5 Stop the engine, replace the spark plug and lead and then repeat the procedure with the other cylinder and carburettor after removing the spark plug from the cylinder which has just been adjusted.

6 The engine will now be running at a high idling speed with both cylinders firing. Hence screw out the throttle valve adjusting screws an EQUAL amount both sides - a fraction of a turn at a time - until the engine idles at approximately 1500 rpm. Note: The pilot screw should always be kept in the range 1½ ± ¼ full turns out.

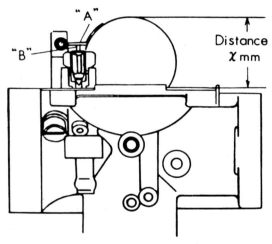

Fig. 2.2. Checking float level

A   Float tongue
B   Float valve
X   27.3 mm

8 Synchronising the carburettors

1 Power output will be unbalanced unless both carburettors work in perfect harmony with each other. Many cases of poor performance and low power output can be traced to carburettors which are out of phase with each other.

2 It is imperative to check that both carburettor slides enter the bore of the carburettor at the same time. Remove the air cleaner hoses and open the throttle wide (engine dead) so that both slides are raised to their maximum height. Slowly close the throttle and check that both slides enter the carburettor bores at the same time. If they do not, make adjustments with either cable adjuster until they are in phase. Check that both slides close fully when the throttle is shut. Reconnect the air filter hoses and run the engine.

3 If carburettor adjustments are required, they should be made BEFORE the carburettors are synchronised. Always make the

synchronising adjustments with the engine warm, to obviate the risk of a false setting.

9 Carburettor settings

1 Some of the carburettor settings, such as the sizes of the needle jets, main jets and needle positions are predetermined by the manufacturer. Under normal circumstances, it is unlikely that these settings will require modification, even though there is provision made. If a change appears necessary, it can often be traced to a developing engine fault.

2 As a rough guide, the slow running screw controls the engine speed up to 1/8 throttle. The throttle valve cutaway controls the engine speed from 1/8 to 1/4 throttle and the position of the needle from 1/4 to 3/4 throttle. The main jet is responsible for the engine speed at the final 3/4 to full throttle. It should be added that none of these demarkation lines is clearly defined; there is a certain amount of overlap between the carburettor components involved.

3 Always err on the side of a rich mixture because a weak mixture has a particularly adverse effect on the running of any two-stroke engine. A weak mixture will cause rapid overheating, which may eventually promote engine seizure. Reference to Chapter 3 will show how the condition of the spark plugs can be used as a reliable guide to carburettor mixture strength.

10 Exhaust system - cleaning

1 The exhaust system is often the most neglected part of any two-stroke despite the fact that it has quite a pronounced effect on performance. It is essential that the exhaust system is inspected and cleaned out at regular intervals because the exhaust gases from a two-stroke engine have a particularly oily nature which will encourage the build-up of sludge. This will cause back pressures and affect the 'breathing' of the engine.

2 Cleaning is made easy by fitting the silencers with detachable baffles, held in position by a setscrew which passes through each silencer end. If the screw is withdrawn, the baffles can be drawn out of position for cleaning.

3 A wash with a petrol/paraffin mix will remove most of the oil and carbon deposits, but if the build-up is severe it is permissible to heat the baffles with a blow lamp and burn off the carbon and old oil.

4 At less frequent intervals, such as when the engine requires decarbonising, it is advisable also to clean out the exhaust pipes. This will prevent the gradual build-up of an internal coating of carbon and oil, over an extended period.

5 Do not run the machine with the baffles detached or with a quite different type of silencers fitted. The standard production silencers have been designed to give the best possible performance whilst subduing the exhaust note. Although a modified exhaust system may give the illusion of greater speed as a result of the changed exhaust note, the chances are that performance will have suffered accordingly.

6 When replacing the exhaust system, use new sealing rings at the exhaust port joints and check that the baffle retaining screws are tightened fully in the silencer ends.

11 Air cleaner - dismantling, servicing and reassembling

1 Before access can be gained to the air cleaner box and hoses it is necessary first to remove the left hand cover which protects the battery and wiring. The air cleaner and box as fitted to the T500J and earlier models are identical. The following procedure should be used as a guide for later models.

2 To remove the air cleaner assembly, detach the two hoses from the carburettor intakes by slackening the retaining clips around the bell mouths. Remove also the two screws which secure the air cleaner assembly to the frame of the machine. The air cleaner will now lift away, complete with hoses.

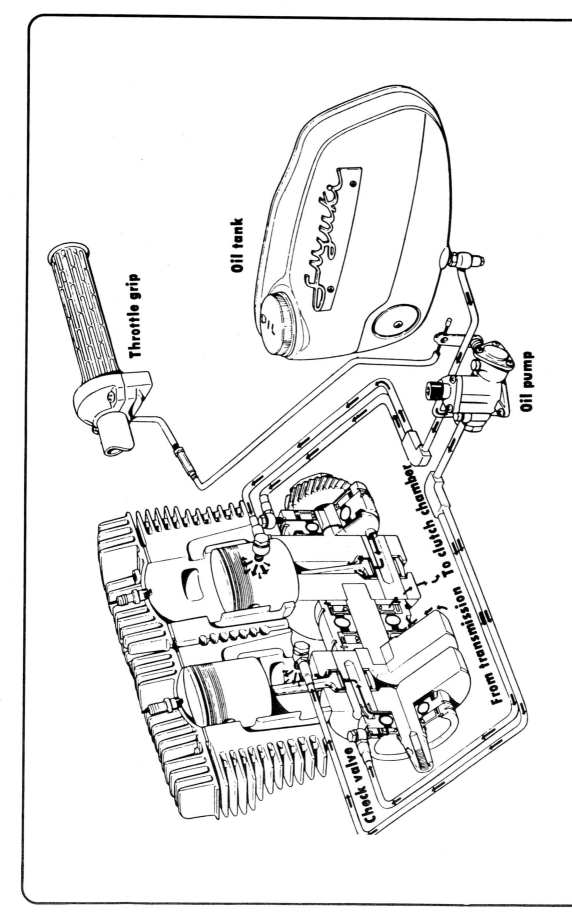

Throttle grip

Oil tank

Oil pump

To clutch chamber

From transmission

Check valve

Fig. 2.3. Diagrammatic illustration of the oil lubricating system

3 The air cleaner element is contained within the air cleaner box. The box is separated by unscrewing the central bolt or butterfly nut and removing the lid and air cleaner element.
4 The T500 model is fitted with a resin-impregnated paper element. This is cleaned by using a jet of compressed air to blow away the accumulation of dust and other foreign matter. Check both the inside and the outside.
5 If the element is damp or badly choked, it is advisable to replace it. A dirty or blocked element will increase the rate of petrol consumption and will cause a marked fall-off in performance.
6 The GT500 A is fitted with an oil-impregnated foam element. Suzuki recommend that the element is cleaned at 2000 mile (3000 km) intervals.
7 To clean the foam element remove it from the air cleaner casing and pull each foam half off the supporting frame. Wash the element in clean petrol to remove the old oil and any dust which has been trapped by it. When it is clean, wrap it in some clean rag and gently squeeze out the remaining petrol. The element should now be left for a while to allow any residual petrol to evaporate. Soak the element in Suzuki CCI oil or a high grade SAE 30 motor oil and then squeeze out any excess to leave the foam damp, but not dripping.
8 Do not run the machine with the air cleaner detached, even for a short period. The carburettors are jetted to compensate for the addition of the air cleaner and the carburation will be upset badly if it is removed. The effect will be overheating as a direct result of the permanently-weakened mixture strength and the risk of subsequent engine damage.
9 The air cleaner is reassembled by reversing the dismantling procedure. If the rubber hoses are split or perished, renew them in order to preclude the possibility of air leaks.

12 Engine lubrication

1 The engine oil is contained in an oil tank mounted on the right hand side of the machine. The tank holds 1.8 litres of oil and is fitted with an oil level inspection 'window' as a precaution against running out.
2 If the oil level falls below the screw in the centre of the inspection window, the tank must be replenished with oil of the correct viscosity. The machine should be standing on level ground when this check is made.
3 Oil flows from the oil tank to the oil pump by gravity, via a banjo union in the main outlet. The base of the outlet is fitted with a detachable cap which contains an integral magnet. This cap must be removed and cleaned during every three-monthly or 2000 mile service.
4 The oil pump is driven by a worm and pinion arrangement from the kickstart shaft in the gearbox. It is of the plunger type and must be replaced as a complete unit if it malfunctions.
5 The oil pump is interconnected to the throttle by means of a spring-loaded operating arm which is actuated by an extra control cable from the throttle cable junction box. Provision is included for bleeding the pump and also for adjusting the setting of the operating arm, as described in Chapter 1, Sections 40.2, and 40.4. This procedure must be followed when the engine is dismantled or if the oil tank is permitted to run dry. Air bubbles will impede the free flow of oil.
6 In order to sustain a positive pressure, each of the oil pipe unions is fitted with a spring-loaded ball valve at the point where they connect with the crankcase drillings. If the ball valves are dismantled, it is essential that they are primed with oil prior to assembly and they are subsequently bled as detailed in Section 40.4 of Chapter 1.
7 A major advantage of the 'Posi-Force' system is the fact that a pressure feed of oil will be maintained even when the throttle is closed. This obviates the risk of engine seizure which is liable to occur with petrol lubricated engines when the machine coasts down a long incline with the throttle closed.

13 Fault diagnosis

Symptom	Reason/s	Remedy
Engine gradually fades and stops	Fuel starvation	Leaking vacuum pipe from carburettor to petrol tap. Replace pipe. Check vent hole in filler cap and clear if blocked. Sediment in filter bowl or blocking float needle. Dismantle and clean.
Engine runs badly, black smoke from exhausts	Carburettors flooding	Dismantle and clean carburettors. Look for punctured float, or for leaking needle valve.
	Ruptured diaphragm in petrol tap	Remove feed pipe and check whether petrol flows when in normal running position. If so, replace diaphragm.
Engine lacks response and overheats	Weak mixture	Check for partial blockage in fuel/carburettors.
	Air cleaner disconnected or hoses split	Reconnect or repair.
White smoke from exhausts	Oil pump setting incorrect; too much oil passing	Check and reset oil pump.
	Incorrect oil in oil tank	Drain and refill with recommended grade.
General lack of response to varying throttle openings.	Blocked exhaust system	Remove silencer baffles and clean.

Chapter 3 Ignition System

Contents

Specifications

Spark plugs

Make	NGK
Type..	B8HS (B7HS alternative)
Gap	0.5 – 0.6 mm (0.020 – 0.024 inch)

Contact breakers

Gap	0.012 in - 0.016 in (0.3 - 0.4 mm) CDI system, GT500A model

Ignition timing	0.134 in (3.44 mm) BTDC both cylinders, measured by dial gauge
	24° BTDC both cylinders, measured by degree disc

Capacitor (condenser)

Rating	0.22 - 0.28 pi F
Resistance	10 + Meg ohm

1 General description

The spark necessary to ignite the petrol/air mix in the combustion chambers is derived from a battery and twin ignition coils. Each cylinder has its own separate contact breaker, condenser and coil to determine the exact moment at which the spark will occur. When the contact breaker points separate the low tension circuit is broken and a high tension voltage is developed by the coil which jumps the air gap across the points of the spark plug and ignites the mixture.

An alternator attached to the left hand end of the crankshaft assembly generates an alternating current which is rectified and used to charge the 12 volt, 7 amp hr battery. The rectifier is located below the nose of the dual seat, on the left hand side of the machine, close to the battery. The twin ignition coils are mounted within the top frame tubes, close to the steering head of the machine. Both contact breakers and their condensers form part of the stator plate assembly which surrounds the generator rotor. The GT500A model has a CDI system, eliminating the need for contact breakers. The circuit is actuated by an ignition switch and key on the left hand side of the machine, immediately below the nose of the petrol tank. This switch also operates the lights for both running and parking.

2 Crankshaft alternator - checking the output

1 The output from the alternator mounted on the end of the crankshaft can be checked only with specialised test equipment of the multi-meter type. It is unlikely that the average owner/rider will have access to this equipment or instruction in its use. In consequence, if the performance of the alternator is in any way suspect, it should be checked by a Suzuki agent or an auto-electrical specialist.

1.2 The twin ignition coils are mounted within the top frame tubes

3 Ignition coils - checking

1 Each ignition coil is a sealed unit, designed to give long service without the need for attention. They are located close together within the two top frame tubes, immediately to the rear of the steering head. If a weak spark and difficult starting cause the performance of either coil to be suspect, have the coils tested by a Suzuki agent or an auto-electrical specialist who will have the appropriate test equipment. A faulty coil must be replaced; it is not possible to effect a satisfactory repair.

2 It is extremely unlikely that both coils will fail on the same occasion. If the complete ignition system fails, it is highly probable that the source of the fault will be found elsewhere. Apart from the common low tension supply, both coils work on independent circuits.

4 Contact breakers - adjustments

All models except GT500A

1 To gain access to the contact breaker assembly it is necessary to detach the left hand crankcase cover by removing the three crosshead screws.

2 Rotate the engine slowly by means of the kickstarter until first one and then the other set of contact breaker points is in the fully-open position. Examine the faces of the contacts. If they are pitted or burnt it will be necessary to remove them for further attention, as described in Section 5 of this Chapter.

3 Adjustment is carried out by slackening the screw which retains the fixed contact plate in position and inserting the point of a screwdriver between the slot in the baseplate and the projecting pegs, so that the contact can be moved in the direction desired. When the contact breaker gap is within the range 0.012 inch to 0.016 inch, as measured with a feeler gauge, tighten the clamp screw and recheck the gap. The feeler gauge must be a good sliding fit.

4 Repeat this adjustment for the second set of contact breaker points, making sure that the gap is EXACTLY identical with that of the other set of points.

5 Before replacing the cover, place a very light smear of grease on the contact breaker cam, making sure that none

reaches the contact surfaces.

5 Contact breaker points - removal, renovation and replacement

All models except GT500A

1 If the contact breaker points are burned, pitted or badly worn, they should be removed for dressing. If it is necessary to remove a substantial amount of material before the faces can be restored, the points should be replaced without question.

2 To remove the contact breaker points, slacken and remove the nut of the moving contact terminal to which the condenser lead is attached. Lift off the condenser lead and also the spring strip of the contact breaker arm, taking note of the way in which the insulating washers are assembled. Failure to observe the method of assembly may result in the contact being earthed inadvertently during reassembly, with the consequent isolation of the contact breaker circuit.

3 Detach the small circlip on the end of the moving contact pivot, using a pair of thin nosed pliers. The moving contact complete with insulating arm, spring and washers can now be removed.

4 The fixed contact together with its mounting plate is removed by withdrawing the one retaining screw.

5 The points should be dressed with an oilstone or fine emery cloth. Keep them absolutely square during the dressing operation otherwise they will make angular contact with each other when they are replaced and will quickly burn away.

6 Replace the contacts by reversing the dismantling procedure, making sure the insulating washers are replaced in the correct order. It is advantageous to apply a thin smear of grease to the moving contact pivot pin, prior to replacement of the contact arm.

7 Re-adjust the contact breaker gap before passing to the second contact breaker assembly. Repeat the dismantling, renovating, reassembly and re-adjustment procedure.

6 Condensers - removal and replacement

All models except GT500A

1 The condensers are included in the contact breaker circuitry to prevent arcing across the contact breaker points when they separate. Each condenser is connected in parallel with its own set of points and if a fault develops, ignition failure will occur in the circuit involved.

2 If the engine is difficult to start or if misfiring occurs on one cylinder, it is possible that the condenser in the ignition circuit of that cylinder has failed. To check, separate the contact breaker points by hand whilst the ignition is switched on. If a spark occurs across the points and they have a blackened and burnt appearance, the condenser can be regarded as unserviceable.

3 It is not possible to check the condenser without the appropriate test equipment. It is best to fit a replacement condenser in view of the low cost involved, and observe the effect on engine performance.

4 Each condenser is attached to the contact breaker baseplate by a screw which passes through an integral clamp. It is necessary to remove also the condenser lead wire attachment to the terminal of the moving contact breaker arm.

5 It is highly improbable that both condensers will fail simultaneously. If this impression is given, commence looking for the source of the trouble in some other part of the ignition circuit.

6 Replace the new condenser by reversing the dismantling procedure. Make sure the clamp screw is tight because this forms the earth connection of the condenser. Check also that the insulating washers at the condenser lead terminal connection are in the correct order, to prevent electrical isolation and the recurrence of arcing across the points.

7 Ignition timing - checking and resetting

1 If the ignition timing is correct, the inscribed lines on the

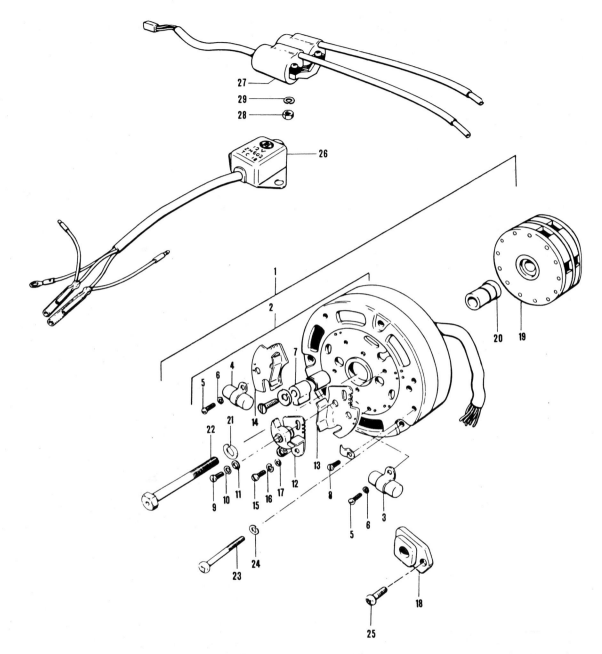

FIG. 3.1. ALTERNATOR AND IGNITION COILS

1	Generator assembly		16	Spring washer (2 off)
2	Stator assembly		17	Washer (2 off)
3	Capacitor (condenser) - RH		18	Wiring harness grommet
4	Capacitor (condenser) - LH		19	Rotor
5	Screw (2 off)		20	Contact breaker cam
6	Spring washer (2 off)		21	Spring washer
7	Oil pad - felt		22	Cam/rotor retaining bolt
8	Screw		23	Screw (3 off)
9	Screw (4 off)		24	Spring washer (3 off)
10	Spring washer (4 off)		25	Screw
11	Washer (4 off)		26	Wattage regulator assembly
12	Contact breaker points assembly (2 off)		27	Ignition coil
13	Contact breaker base plate - RH		28	Nut (2 off)
14	Contact breaker base plate - LH		29	Spring washer (2 off)
15	Screw (2 off)			

on the accuracy with which the ignition timing is set. Even a small error can cause a marked reduction in performance and the possibility of engine damage, particularly to the pistons. Although alignment of the rotor - stator timing marks will verify whether the timing is accurate within certain limits, it is preferable to cross-check with a dial gauge and timing tester - the latter may simply consist of a small battery and bulb connected across the points with crocodile clips. Insert the dial gauge through the spark plug hole in the left hand cylinder head and set the ignition timing so that the points commence to separate when the piston is 3.4 mm (0.134 inch) before top dead centre. The timing tester will show when the points have broken contact. Repeat this procedure for the right hand cylinder.

2   For those who prefer to use a timing disc attached to the end of the crankshaft, the corresponding setting is 24° before top dead centre.

3   If the ignition timing is correct, the inscribed lines on the rotor of the alternator will coincide EXACTLY with the line inscribed on the fixed stator plate as the contact breaker points for the cylinder concerned are on the point of separation.

4   The black line - or line stamped R - on the rotor applies to the timing of the right hand cylinder (right hand set of points). The red line - or line stamped L - on the rotor applies to the timing of the left hand cylinder (left hand set of points).

5   Before checking or resetting the ignition timing, always ensure the contact breaker gaps are correct. If the gaps are altered after the timing has been checked, some variation of the accuracy of the ignition timing will be inevitable.

6   If the timing is incorrect, the position of the contact breaker points in relation to the contact breaker cam can be adjusted within fixed limits. It is necessary to slacken the baseplate screws and move the complete points assembly in the direction required, using a screwdriver between the slots at the extreme edge of the baseplate and the projecting pegs close by. Retighten the baseplate screws when the timing adjustment is correct, and check again.

7   The contact breaker circuit does not contain any provision for either advancing or retarding the ignition timing whilst the engine is running.

8   The GT500A model has a CDI system, obviating the need for twin contact breakers. On these models, the ignition timing must be checked with a stroboscope.

7.2a Aligning the right hand ...

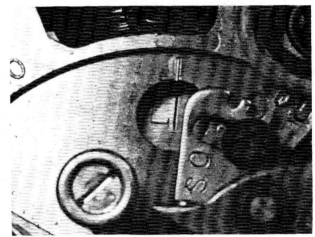

7.2b ... and left hand timing marks

8 Spark plugs - checking and resetting the gaps

1   A matched pair of 14 mm thread diameter, 12.7 mm reach, spark plugs should be fitted. The current plug recommendation is an NGK B8HS plug, with a B7HS alternative. This supersedes the original equipment NGK B-77HC plug which is no longer available.

2   Certain operating conditions may dictate a change of plug grade. If the motorcycle is used for low speed riding and the plugs 'oil up', leading to misfiring, fit the B7HS hotter alternative.

3   Pull the insulating caps off the spark plugs and make sure you identify which HT lead goes to which plug. Use a spark plug socket to remove the plugs from the cylinder head. The hex size of the plugs is 20.8 mm.

4   Clean the plug with a wire brush to remove carbon deposits. The correct gap between the plug electrodes is 0.5 – 0.6 mm (0.020 – 0.024 inch). Use feeler gauges to measure the plug gap and if necessary adjust it by bending the outer (earth) electrode only. Never bend the centre electrode. Check the plug gaps every 2000 miles or every three months.

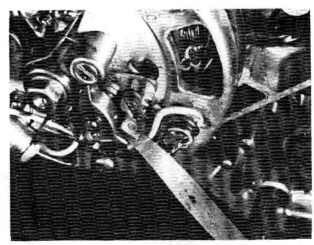

7.3 Ensure the points are fully open when checking the gap

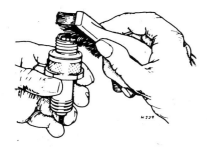

Cleaning deposits from electrodes and surrounding area using a fine wire brush.

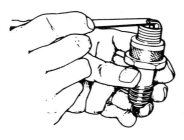

Checking plug gap with feeler gauges

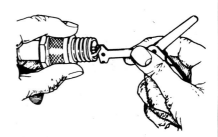

Altering the plug gap. Note use of correct tool.

Fig. 3.2 Spark plug maintenance

White deposits and damaged porcelain insulation indicating overheating

Broken porcelain insulation due to bent central electrode

Electrodes burnt away due to wrong heat value or chronic pre-ignition (pinking)

Excessive black deposits caused by over-rich mixture or wrong heat value

Mild white deposits and electrode burnt indicating too weak a fuel mixture

Plug in sound condition with light greyish brown deposits

Example of spark plug conditions

5 The condition of the spark plug electrodes and insulator can be used as a reliable guide to engine operating conditions, with some experience. See the accompanying diagram.

6 To guard against the rare event of plug failure, always carry a spare pair of spark plugs of the correct grade.

7 Beware of overtightening the spark plugs, otherwise there is risk of stripping the threads from the aluminium alloy cylinder heads. The plugs should be sufficiently tight to seat firmly on their copper sealing washers and no more. Use a spanner which is a good fit, to prevent the spanner from slipping and breaking the insulator.

8 If the threads in the cylinder heads strip as a result of over-tightening the spark plugs it is possible to reclaim the heads by the use of a Helicoil thread insert. This is a cheap and convenient way of replacing the threads; many motor cycle dealers operate a service of this nature specifically for 14 mm inserts.

9 Make sure the plug insulating caps are a good fit and have their rubber seals. These caps contain the suppressors which eliminate both radio and TV interference.

7.4 The alternator and contact breaker assembly complete

9 Fault diagnosis

Symptom	Reason/s	Remedy
Engine will not start	Discharged battery	Recharge battery with a battery charger. (If the symptoms return after a short period, have the alternator output and the battery checked).
	Short circuit in wiring system	Check wiring to locate source of fault.
	Break in wiring system	Check wiring to locate break.
	Plug oiled	Replace or clean.
	Dirty/damp points	Clean/dry.
	Blown fuse	Replace fuse.
Engine misfires and eventually stops	Whiskered spark plugs	Replace plugs, using a hotter grade.
	Oiled spark plugs	Replace plugs, using a 'softer' grade.
	Condenser breakdown (except GT500A)	Replace condenser.
	Points pitted (except GT500A)	Replace points and re-set ignition.
	Coil failure	Replace coil.
Engine lacks response and overheats	Reduced contact breaker gaps (except GT500A)	Check and reset gaps.
Engine 'fades' when under heavy load	Pre-ignition	Replace plugs, using only recommended grades.
Engine 'pinks' under load	Ignition advanced	Reset ignition timing.

Chapter 4 Frame and Forks

Contents

1 General description

The various Suzuki 500 cc models have frames and forks which are basically similar. The most noticeable mechanical differences are as follows:

a) Lower fork yoke pinch bolt position.
b) Method of mounting the speedometer and tachometer to the upper fork yoke.
c) Front mudguard stays mounting position.

These variations should not affect the stripdown procedures.

The front forks are of the telescopic type, with oil-filled one-way damper units. The frame is the full cradle type employing duplex tubes. Rear suspension is provided by a swinging arm fork, controlled by hydraulically-damped, adjustable rear suspension units.

2 Front forks - removal from the frame

1 It is unlikely that the front forks will need to be removed from the frame as a complete unit unless the steering head bearings require attention or the forks are damaged in an accident.

2 Commence operations by removing either the control cables from the handlebar control levers or the levers complete with cables. The shape of the handlebars fitted and the length of the control cables will probably dictate which method is used.

3 Detach the handlebars by removing the handlebar clamps, either side of the steering damper. The clamps are each retained by two bolts. Note that the mountings pass through rubber bushes in the top yoke of the forks, which act as a vibration damper. They are each retained by a castellated nut and washer which can be detached after the split pin has been removed.

4 If it is required to dismantle the steering damper, remove the spring clip from the extreme bottom end of the steering damper rod and unscrew the damper knob until it lifts clear complete with the rod attached. Detach also the headlamp complete which is held to the upper fork shrouds by two bolts, one either side.

5 If the machine is equipped with a centre stand, the front wheel may be elevated by placing a block of wood under the stand. Alternatively, balance the machine such that the bottom frames tubes are resting on a suitably sized solid object (eg a wooden box or a breeze block and wood support) such that the front wheel is well clear of the ground.

6 Remove the speedometer drive cable from the gearbox in the

front hub by unscrewing the round coupling nut. Detach also the front brake cable by unscrewing the adjusting nut and withdrawing the cable together with its outer cable adjuster and rubber gaiter from the brake hub anchorage. The wheel can now be released from the forks by unscrewing the clamp bolt through the bottom of the right hand fork leg and withdrawing the wheel spindle which has two flats on the end to accept a spanner. The spindle will unscrew from the left hand fork leg and pull clear.

7   Remove the front wheel complete with brake plate assembly. If desired, the front mudguard can be removed at this stage. On earlier models, this may be achieved by detaching the nuts and bolts which retain the fork stays to the lugs on the lower fork legs and the two bolts on either side of the mudguard bridge which thread into the lower fork legs. On later models, remove the two bolts on either side of the mudguard bridge. Subsequently, free both the speedometer cable and the brake cable from the guide attached to the lower left hand end of the front mudguard and from the cable clips on the bottom yoke of the telescopic forks. These clamps are bent easily without disturbing the retaining bolts.

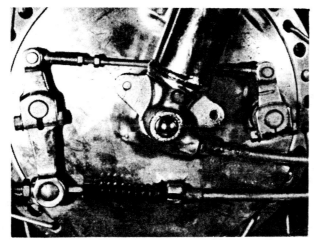

2.6 Remove the speedometer cable and front brake cable

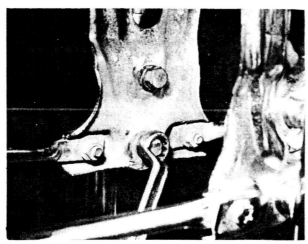

2.7 The mudguard is held by two bolts inside each fork leg

8   Unscrew the large diameter nut in the centre of the top yoke of the forks and remove it together with washer and clip which bears on the inside of the steering damper knob. Detach the speedometer drive cable and the tachometer drive cable from their respective indicators and remove both of the large bolts which thread into the top of each fork leg. The bolts will release an O ring seal and a seating washer.

9   The top yoke of the forks can now be pulled clear together with the speedometer and tachometer heads, and the flashing indicator lamps.

10   Whilst the forks are supported in position, remove the steering head locknut and washer. The locknut is slotted, to facilitate the use of a C spanner. The forks are now completely free and can be withdrawn from the bottom of the steering head stem. It may be necessary to raise the machine even higher so that they can be pulled clear of the frame completely.

11   Note that when the forks are removed from the frame, the uncaged ball bearings in the top and bottom steering head races are liable to fall free. It is advisable to wrap some rag around each race as it separates, to trap the bearings as they work free.

3   Front forks - dismantling

1   It is advisable to dismantle each fork leg separately, using an identical procedure. There is less chance of unwittingly inter-changing parts if this approach is adopted. Commence by draining the forks; there is a drain screw in each leg, above the wheel spindle.

2   Slacken the pinch bolt through the lower yoke and withdraw the fork leg assembly complete. Remove the upper gaiter support, the rubber gaiter, the spring, the dust seal and the spring seating.

3   Unscrew the chromium plated collar which threads onto the lower outer leg of the forks. This collar has a normal right hand thread and should not prove too difficult to unscrew if the fork leg is held in a vice. A wide rubber band, or a piece of old inner tube, around the collar will improve the grip; in an extreme case this may be augmented by a strap or a chain wrench.

4   Remove the collar and withdraw the inner fork tube complete with limit ring and lower bush. The top bush and O ring seal will be a sliding fit over the inner fork tube after they have been released from the top of the lower fork leg by the screwed collar. The fork leg is now dismantled completely, leaving the headlamp and top fork shrouds in position. Repeat this procedure for the other fork leg.

5   If it is desired to dismantle either or both fork legs without disturbing the steering head races, follow the procedure given in the preceding Section from paragraphs 5 to 7 inclusive. Then continue from paragraph 2 of this Section, after first removing the large chromium plated bolt which threads into the top of the fork leg, through the top yoke of the forks.

6   On the GT500A models, there is no screwed collar. On these models raise the rubber boot and detach the circlip within the lower fork leg, which will permit the fork tube to be withdrawn. DO NOT release the bolt recessed into the wheel spindle cut-out which centres the spring seating. Loosening the bolt will misalign the seat and cause the forks to chatter or rattle on reassembly.

3.2a Slacken the pinch bolt through the lower fork yoke

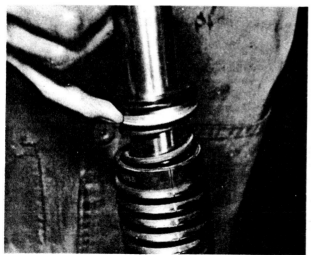

3.2b Remove the upper gaiter support ...

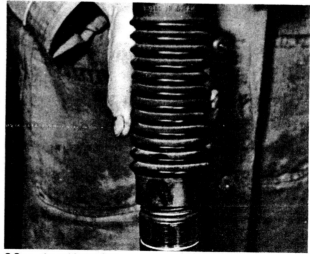

3.2c ... the rubber gaiter ...

3.2d ... the spring ...

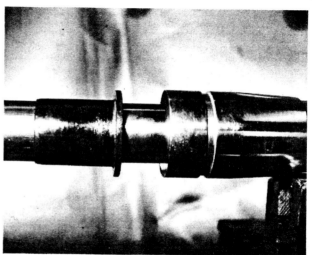

3.2e ... the dust seal

3.3 Slacken threaded collar by using a piece of old inner tube and a chain wrench

3.4a Removing the inner fork tube complete with upper bush and limit ring ...

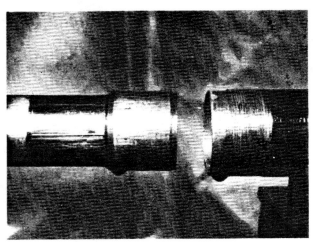

3.4b ... and lower bush

4 Steering head bearings - examination and renovation

1   Before commencing reassembly of the forks, examine the steering head races. The ball bearing tracks of the respective cup and cone bearings should be polished and free from indentations or cracks. If signs of wear or damage are evident, the cups and cones must be replaced. They are a tight push fit and should be drifted out of position.
2   Ball bearings are cheap. If the originals are marked or discoloured, they should be replaced without question. To hold the steel balls in position during re-attachment of the forks, pack the bearings with grease. Note that each race should have space to include one extra ball. This space is necessary to prevent the ball bearings from skidding on each other, which would accelerate the rate of wear.

5 Front forks - examination and renovation

1   The parts most liable to wear over an extended period of service are the bushes which fit over the inner tubes of each fork leg and the oil seals contained within each screwed collar. Worn fork bushes normally cause judder when the front brake is applied and the increased amount of play can be detected by pulling and pushing on the handlebars when the front brake is full on.
2   Replacement of the worn bushes is quite straightforward. The upper bush fits under the screwed collar of the lower outer fork leg and acts mainly as a guide for the fork inner tube. It has an O ring seal between its upper lip and the screwed collar, to prevent oil leakage.
3   The lower bush is permanently attached to the bottom end of the fork inner tube by means of a peg. Specialist attention is required when this bush wears and it is recommended that the replacement is fitted by a Suzuki agent.
4   The main oil seal is housed in the screwed collar. If the seal shows signs of deterioration it should be replaced. This may be achieved by drifting the oil seal out through the non-tapered end of the collar. The replacement of the new oil seal merely involves the reversal of this procedure. However, this is a delicate operation and, once again, it is recommended that the replacement is fitted by a Suzuki agent.
5   Check the fork springs for wear. If wear is evident, or if the springs have taken a permanent set, they must be replaced, always as a pair.
6   Check the outer surface of the fork inner tubes for scratches or roughness. It is only too easy to damage the main oil seal during reassembly, if this precaution is not observed. Light scratches may be removed with very fine emery paper; deep

scratches will necessitate the renewal of the fork tube.
7   Inspect also the dust seals, on which the bottom of each fork spring seats. If the seals are damaged, they will permit the ingress of foreign matter, which will impair fork efficiency.
8   It is rarely possible to straighten forks which have been bent as the result of accident damage, especially if the correct jigs are not available. It is always advisable to err on the safe side and fit new replacements, especially since there is no means of checking to what extent the damaged forks have been overstressed.
9   Damping is effected by oil within each fork leg passing either in or out of small holes drilled in the fork leg itself. The damping action can be altered by changing the viscosity of the oil, although a change is unlikely to prove necessary in most cases.

6 Front forks - replacement

1   Replace the front forks by reversing either of the dismantling procedures described in Sections 2 and 3 of this Chapter, whichever is the more appropriate. Make sure the brake plate locates with the projection on the fork leg.
2   Before fully tightening the front wheel spindle, fork yoke pinch bolts and the bolts in the top of each fork leg, bounce the forks several times to ensure they work freely and are clamped in their original settings. Complete the final tightening from the front wheel spindle upwards.
3   Do not forget to add fork oil before the bolts in the top of each fork leg are tightened. Each fork leg requires the same amount of fork oil; use 10, 15 or 20W fork oil as preferred. On T500 models the quantity is 220 cc and on GT500A models the quantity is 266 cc. Check that the drain plug has been replaced in the bottom of each fork leg before the oil is added!

6.3 Use an oil syringe to fill the forks with oil

4   Difficulty is often experienced when attempting to draw the fork inner tube into position in the top yoke, during reassembly. It is worthwhile making up a special tool to aid the correct location, which takes the form of a threaded rod of the correct diameter, to which a T handle is attached.
5   Check the adjustment of the steering head bearings before the machine is used on the road and again shortly afterwards. If the bearings are too slack, fork judder will occur. There should be no play at the head races when the handlebars are pushed and pulled with the front brake applied hard.
6   Overtight head races are equally undesirable. It is possible to place a pressure of several tons on the head bearings by overtightening, even though the handlebars seem to turn freely. Overtight head bearings will cause the machine to roll at low speeds and give imprecise steering. Adjustment is correct if there is no play in the bearings and the handlebars swing to full lock

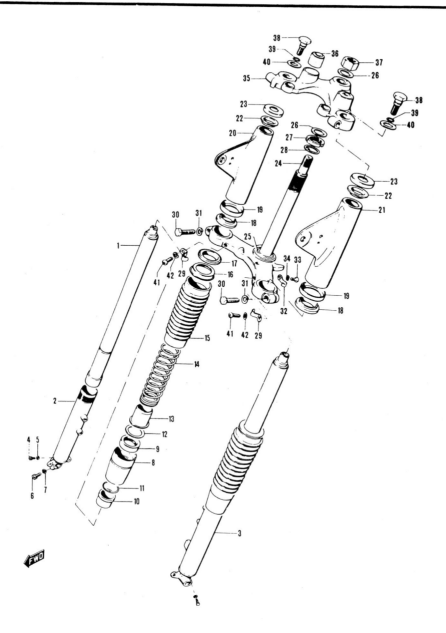

FIG. 4.1. FRONT FORKS (EXCEPT T500)

1 Fork inner tube (2 off)	22 Upper shroud cushion (2 off)
2 Right hand outer tube	23 Upper shroud seat (2 off)
3 Left hand outer tube	24 Lower fork yoke/steering stem
4 Drain plug (2 off)	25 Ball race - outer
5 Drain plug washer (2 off)	26 Steering head stem washer
6 Pinch bolt	27 Steering head stem locknut
7 Spring washer	28 Steering head stem lock washer
8 Outer tube threaded collar (2 off)	29 Speedometer cable clip (2 off)
9 Oil seal (2 off)	30 Bottom yoke pinch bolt (2 off)
10 Inner tube guide bush (2 off)	31 Spring washer (2 off)
11 'O' ring seal (2 off)	32 Brake cable clip
12 Spring seating (2 off)	33 Screw
13 Dust seal (2 off)	34 Spring washer
14 Spring (2 off)	35 Top fork yoke
15 Rubber gaiter (2 off)	36 Handlebar rubber mountings (2 off)
16 Gaiter support (2 off)	37 Top yoke retaining nut
17 Spring seating (2 off)	38 Fork top bolt (2 off)
18 Shroud cushion (2 off)	39 'O' ring seal (2 off)
19 Shroud seat (2 off)	40 Flat washer (2 off)
20 Right hand fork shroud	41 Crosshead screw (2 off)
21 Left hand fork shroud	42 Spring washer (2 off)

either side when the machine is on the centre stand with the front wheel clear of the ground. Only a light tap on each end should cause the handlebars to swing. Ensure that the steering damper is not operating when setting up the head bearings.

7 Steering head lock

1 The steering head lock is attached to the upper surface of the lower fork yoke by two screws. When in the locked position, a plunger is lowered, which falls between two projections cast in the yoke when the handlebars are on full left hand lock. The handlebars cannot be straightened until the lock is released and the plunger raised.
2 If the lock malfunctions, it must be replaced. A repair is impracticable. When the lock is changed it follows that the key must be changed too, to match the new lock.

8 Steering damper - function and use

1 A steering damper is a fitting which provides means of adding friction to the steering head assembly so that the front forks will turn less easily. It is a relic of the early days of motor cycling when machines were liable to develop 'speed wobbles' which grew in intensity until the rider was unseated. With today's more sophisticated front fork damping and improved frame designs, a steering damper is almost a superfluous fitting unless a sidecar is attached to the machine or very poor road surfaces are encountered.
2 The steering damper is, in effect, a small clutch without any compression springs. When the steering damper knob is tightened, the friction discs and the plain discs are brought into closer proximity with each other and it is more difficult to deflect the handlebars from their set position. If the knob is tightened fully, the handlebars are virtually locked in position. Under normal riding conditions, the steering damper should be slackened off. Only at very high speeds or on rough surfaces is there any need to apply some damper friction.
3 The steering damper assembly will be found at the base of the steering head column, immediately below the bottom fork yoke. The centre fixed plate is attached to the yoke by the left hand lock stop.
4 Although it is unlikely that the steering damper assembly will require attention during the normal service life of the machine, it can be removed by withdrawing the damper knob and threaded rod, following the procedure given in Section 2.4 of this Chapter. The remainder of the assembly is freed when the left hand lock stop of the bottom fork yoke is unscrewed.

9 Frame - examination and renovation

1 The frame is unlikely to require attention unless accident damage has occurred. In some cases, replacement of the frame is the only satisfactory course of action if it is out of alignment. Only a few frame repair specialists will have the necessary jigs and mandrels essential for resetting the frame and even then there is no means of assessing to what extent the frame may have been overstressed.
2 After a machine has covered an extensive mileage, it is advisable to inspect the frame for signs of cracking or splitting at any of the welded joints. Rust corrosion can also cause weaknesses at these joints. Minor repairs can be affected by welding or brazing, depending on the extent of the damage.
3 Remember that a frame which is out of alignment will cause handling problems and may even promote the 'speed wobbles'. If misalignment is suspected, as the result of an accident, it will be necessary to strip the machine completely so that the frame can be checked and, if needs be, replaced.

10 Swinging arm rear fork - dismantling, examination and renovation

1 The rear fork of the frame assembly pivots on a detachable bush within each end of the fork crossmember and a pivot which passes through frame lugs and the centre of each of the two bushes. It is quite easy to renovate the swinging arm pivots when wear necessitates attention.
2 To remove the swinging arm fork, first detach the rear chainguard and the final drive chain. The former is retained by a countersunk crosshead screw in front of the mounting for the bottom of the left hand rear suspension unit and by a bolt through a lug which locates with the inner portion of the fork crossmember, on the left hand end of the radiused section. It is best to separate the chain whilst the spring link is resting on the rear wheel sprocket.
3 Detach the rear brake torque arm from the brake plate by removing the spring clip and withdrawing the securing nut, washer and bolt. Remove also the cable from the brake arm. Then withdraw the rear brake cable by unscrewing the adjuster from the brake plate and freeing the rear wheel complete with sprocket and brake drum by unscrewing the inner of the two left hand spindle nuts, withdrawing the wheel spindle, then removing the large diameter left hand nut. Do not lose the distance piece which will fall clear from the right hand side of the wheel as it is removed.
4 Remove both rear suspension units from their rear fork mountings. Each is retained in position by a domed nut and a washer. When the nuts and washers have been removed, the units can be pulled off their mounting studs.
5 Remove the self-locking nut from the left hand end of the swinging arm pivot pin. Withdraw the pin and pull the swinging arm fork from the frame.
6 If the dust cap is removed from each end of the fork crossmember, the O ring seal, thrust washer and the pivot bearing bush can be withdrawn. Three separate spacers are carried between the two bearing bushes; these should be removed and the outer spacers inspected for wear.
7 Wear will take place in the bearing bushes, both of which should be replaced. Replace both the bearing bushes and the pivot pin if the clearance between them exceeds 0.014 inch (0.35 mm) or the pivot pin if it is out of true by more than 0.020 inch (0.5 mm).
8 Reassemble the swinging arm fork by reversing the dismantling procedure. Grease the pivot pin and both steering bushes liberally prior to reassembly and check that the grease nipple fitted in the top crossmember of the fork is not obstructed.
9 Worn swinging arm pivot bearings will give imprecise handling with a tendency for the rear of the machine to twitch or hop. The play can be detected by placing the machine on its centre stand and with the rear wheel clear of the ground pushing and pulling sideways on the fork ends.

11 Rear suspension units - examination

1 Rear suspension units of the hydraulically-damped type are fitted to all the Suzuki 500 cc twins. They can be adjusted to give three different spring settings, without removal from the machine.
2 Each rear suspension unit has two peg holes immediately above the adjusting notches, to facilitate adjustment. Either a C spanner or a metal rod can be used to turn the adjusters. Turn clockwise (looking from the top) to increase the spring tension and stiffen up the suspension. The recommended settings are as follows:

Position 1 (least tension)	Normal running without a pillion passenger
Position 2 (middle setting)	High speed touring
Position 3 (highest tension)	High speed competition events or with pillion passenger and/or heavy loads

3 There is no means of draining or topping up. If the damping of the suspension units fails, the units complete must be replaced.

4 In the interests of good roadholding it is essential that both suspension units have the same load setting.

12 Centre stand - examination

1 The centre stand is attached to lugs welded to the bottom frame tubes, and pivots on two bushes, one through each leg, which are retained by nuts and bolts. An extension spring is used to keep the stand in the fully-retracted position when the machine is in use.

2 Check that the return spring is in good condition and that both nuts and bolts at the pivots are tight. If the stand falls whilst the machine is in motion it may catch in some obstacle and unseat the rider.

13 Prop stand - examination

1 A prop stand is also fitted, when it is not desired to use the centre stand. The prop stand pivots from a metal plate attached to a lug on the lower left hand frame tube by two bolts and is

10.4 Note the washer between the suspension unit bush and the frame

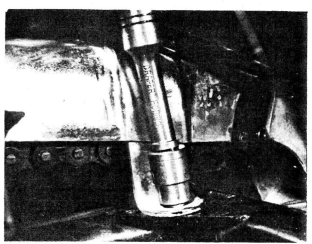

10.2 Removing the bolt which retains the forward end of the chainguard

10.5 Swinging arm pivot pin self-locking nut and washer

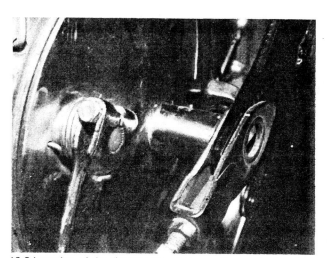

10.3 Location of the distance piece between the rear brake plate and the rear fork end

10.6a Dust cap contains the 'O' ring seal and thrust washer

10.6b Worn outer spacer resulting from lack of greasing

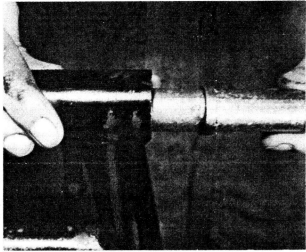

10.8a First insert the central spacer ...

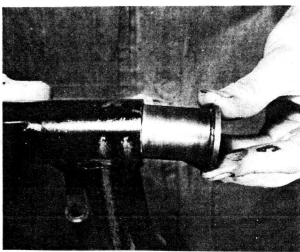

10.8b ... followed by the outer bushes

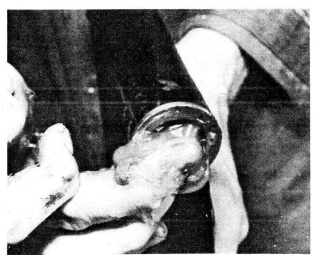

10.8c ... grease well ...

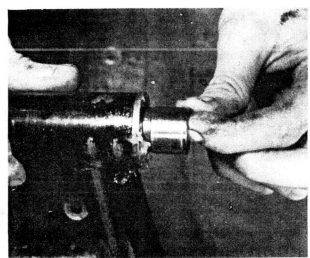

10.8d ... and insert the inner spacers

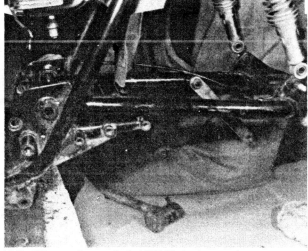

10.8e Offer up the rear fork ABOVE the footrest lugs

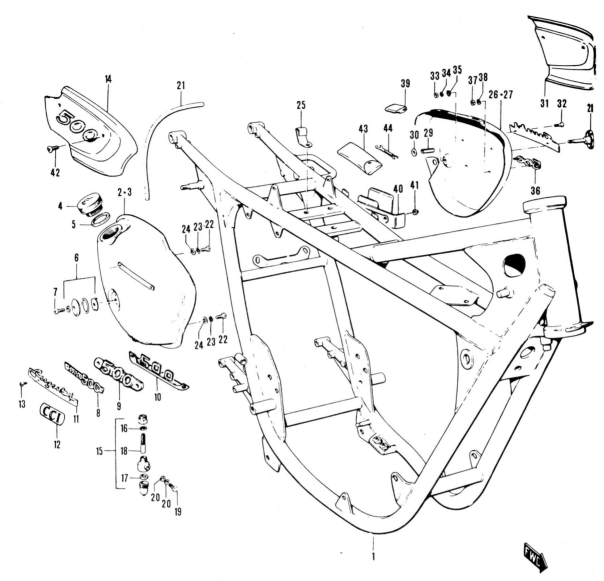

FIG. 4.2. FRAME AND OIL TANK

1	Frame	23	Spring washer (3 off)
2	Oil tank (pre T500R)	24	Washer (3 off)
3	Oil tank (T500R ON)	25	Breather pipe clamp
4	Oil tank cap	26	Battery cover (pre T500R)
5	Cap gasket	27	Battery cover (T500R ON)
6	Oil level lens assembly	28	Battery cover retaining bolt
7	Crosshead screw	29	Cover spacer
8	Emblem (T500 II and T500 III) (2 off)	30	Retainer for 28 and 29
9	Emblem (T500R and T500J) (2 off)	31	Emblem (T500R)
10	Emblem (T500K) (2 off)	32	Crosshead screw (2 off)
11	Emblem (T500) (2 off)	33	Nut (2 off)
12	Emblem (T500R ON) (2 off)	34	Spring washer (2 off)
13	Crosshead screw (2 off)	35	Washer (T500J) (2 off)
14	Emblem (T500J)	36	Emblem (T500)
15	Oil tank outlet assembly	37	Nut (T500) (2 off)
16	Washer	38	Spring washer (T 500) (2 off)
17	Washer	39	Battery cover cushion
18	Oil filter	40	Tool holder/battery retainer
19	Union bolt	41	Nut
20	Washer (2 off)	42	Screw (T500J) (2 off)
21	Oil breather pipe	43	Tool set
22	Oil tank retaining bolt (3 off)	44	Points spanner

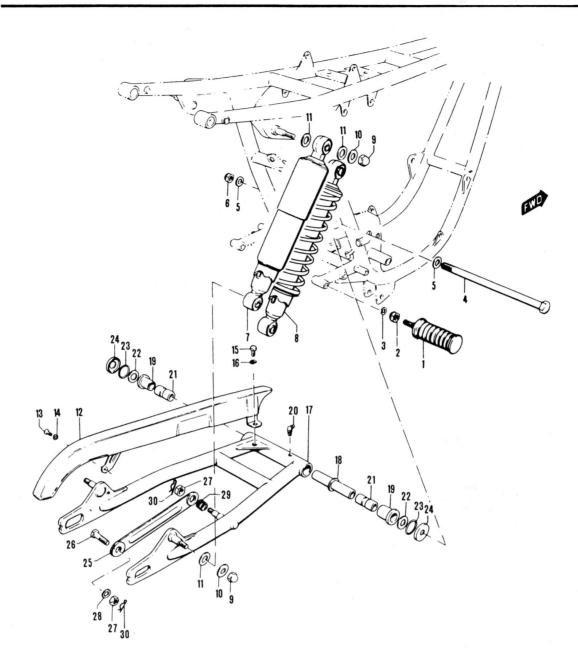

FIG. 4.3. SWINGING ARM SUB FRAME

1	Pillion footrest assembly (2 off)	16	Spring washer
2	Footrest retaining nut (2 off)	17	Swinging arm assembly
3	Spring washer (2 off)	18	Spacer
4	Swinging arm pivot pin	19	Outer bush (2 off)
5	Washer (2 off)	20	Grease nipple
6	Pivot pin nut	21	Inner bush (2 off)
7	Rear suspension unit (T500) (2 off)	22	Thrust washer (2 off)
8	Rear suspension unit (T500 II ON) (2 off)	23	'O' ring seal (2 off)
9	Domed nut (4 off)	24	Dust cover (2 off)
10	Washer (4 off)	25	Rear brake torque arm
11	Washer (6 off)	26	Torque arm bolt
12	Chaincase	27	Nut (2 off)
13	Countersunk screw	28	Spring washer
14	Serrated washer	29	Torque arm spring
15	Bolt	30	Torque arm clip (2 off)

fitted with an extension spring to ensure the stand is retracted automatically immediately the weight of the machine is taken from it.

2 Check that the two bolts retaining the metal plate are both fully tightened and also the single pivot bolt through the eye of the stand arm. Check also that the extension spring is in good condition and is not overstretched. An accident is almost inevitable if the stand extends whilst the machine is on the move!

14 Footrests - examination and renovation

1 Each footrest is bolted to a boss on the plate welded to each of the duplex frame tubes. They are non-adjustable for height and are prevented from turning by a second bolt which passes through an extension of the footrest arm into the tube which extends from each frame tube.

2 If the machine is dropped, it is probable that the rearmost bolt will shear and it will be necessary to drill out the stump after the footrest itself has been removed. If the footrest arm is bent, it can be straightened in a vice, using a blow lamp to warm the area where the bend occurs. The footrest rubber must be removed before any heat is applied.

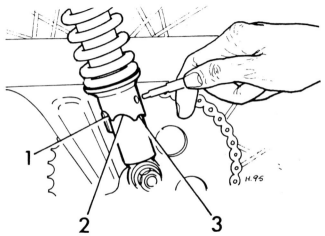

FIG. 4.4. SETTINGS FOR REAR SUSPENSION UNITS

1   Normal riding
2   High speed - solo
3   With pillion riding

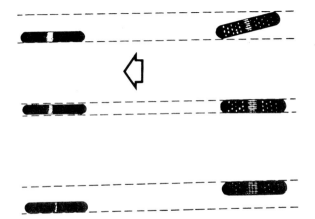

Fig. 4.5. Method of checking wheel alignment

15 Rear brake pedal - examination and renovation

1 The rear brake pedal pivots around a boss attached to the right hand frame tube. It is held captive by the bolt which passes through the right hand footrest, into the centre of the pivot boss. A coil spring around the pivot aids the return of the pedal to its normal operating position.

2 If the brake pedal is bent or twisted in an accident, it should be removed and straightened in a manner similar to that recommended for the footrests in the preceding Section.

16 Dual seat - removal and replacement

1 The dual seat is attached to the rear of the top frame tubes by a bracket with slotted ends. The nose of the seat locates with a tube across the top tubes of the frame, which is raised on two lugs.

2 To remove the dual seat, slacken each of the two nuts at the end bracket and withdraw the seat from the rear. It is replaced bracket with the nuts at the rear of the top frame tubes, which should then be tightened fully.

17 Speedometer and tachometer heads - removal and replacement

1 The speedometer and tachometer heads are mounted on a plate which bolts to the top fork yoke - except in the case of the T500 where the instruments fit within the alloy casting of the top yoke. In either case, the heads are attached by nuts and washers which thread onto studs projecting from the base of each outer instrument case.

2 Before either head can be removed, it is also necessary to detach the drive cables. Unscrew the circular coupling nut from the underside of each head and pull away the cables.

3 In addition, detach the various internal bulbs, which are mounted in rubber-covered bulb holders which push into the base of each instrument.

4 The heads can now be pulled clear from their mountings. The earlier instruments have a rubber cushioning mat to dampen out the effects of vibration. These also will be freed and should not be lost.

5 Apart from defects in either the drive or the drive cable, a speedometer or tachometer which malfunctions is difficult to repair. Fit a replacement, or alternatively, entrust the repair to a competent instrument repair specialist.

6 Remember that a speedometer in correct working order is a statutory requirement in the UK. Apart from this legal requirement, reference to the odometer reading is the best means of keeping pace with the maintenance schedules.

18 Speedometer and tachometer drive cables - examination and maintenance

1 It is advisable to detach both cables from time to time in order to check whether they are lubricated adequately, and whether the outer coverings are compressed or damaged at any point along their run. Jerky or sluggish movements can often be attributed to a cable fault.

2 For greasing, withdraw the inner cable. After removing the old grease, clean with a petrol-soaked rag and examine the cable for broken strands or other damage.

3 Regrease the cable with high melting point grease, taking care not to grease the last six inches at the point where the cable enters the instrument head. If this precaution is not observed, grease will work into the head and immobilise the movement.

4 If either instrument head stops working, suspect a broken drive cable. Inspection will show whether the inner cable has

f so, the inner cable alone can be renewed and re-
n the outer casing, after greasing. Never fit a new inner
ne if the outer covering is damaged or compressed at

18.0 Tachometer drive is taken from the oil pump

any point along its run.

19 Speedometer and tachometer drives - location and examination

1 The speedometer drive gearbox is an integral part of the front wheel brake plate, and is driven internally from the wheel hub. The gearbox rarely gives trouble if it is lubricated regularly. If wear in the drive mechanism occurs, the worm can be withdrawn, complete with shaft, from the brake plate housing. The drive pinion which mates with the worm is secured within the brake plate also, by a circlip in front of the shaped driving plate which engages with slots in the front wheel hub.

2 The tachometer drive is taken from the oil pump, which shares a common drive facility. It is unlikely that the tachometer drive will give trouble.

20 Cleaning the machine

1 After removing all surface dirt with a rag or sponge which is washed frequently in clean water, the machine should be allowed to dry thoroughly. Application of car polish or wax to the cycle parts will give a good finish, particularly if the machine has not been neglected for a long period.

2 The plated parts of the machine should require only a wipe with a damp rag. If the plated parts are badly corroded, as may occur during winter when the roads are salted, it is permissible to use one of the proprietary chrome cleaners. These often have an oily base, which will help to prevent corrosion recurring.

3 If the engine parts are particularly oily, use a cleaning compound such as Gunk or Jizer. Apply the compound whilst the parts are dry and work it in with a brush so that it has the opportunity to penetrate the film of grease and oil. Finish off by washing down liberally, taking care that water does not enter either the carburettors or the electrics. If desired, the now clean, polished aluminium alloy parts can be enhanced further by using a special polish such as Solvol Autosol which will restore them to full lustre.

4 If possible, the machine should be wiped over immediately after it has been used in the wet, so that it is not garaged in damp conditions which will promote rusting. Make sure to wipe the chain and re-oil it, to prevent water from entering the rollers and causing harshness with an accompanying rapid rate of wear. Remember there is little chance of water entering the control cables and causing stiffness of operation, if they are lubricated regularly as recommended in the Routine Maintenance Section.

21 Fault diagnosis

Symptom	Reason/s	Remedy
Machine veers either to the right or the left with hands off handlebars	Incorrect wheel alignment	Check and re-align.
	Bent frame	Check, and if necessary, replace.
	Twisted forks	Check, and if necessary, replace.
Machine rolls at low speeds	Overtight steering head bearings	Slacken bearings.
Machine judders when front brake is applied	Slack steering head bearings	Tighten until all free play is lost.
	Worn fork bushes	Replace bushes.
Machine pitches badly on uneven surfaces	Ineffective front fork dampers	Check oil content of forks.
	Ineffective rear suspension units	Check whether units still have damping action.
Fork action stiff	Fork legs out of alignment (twisted in yokes)	Slacken yoke clamps, front wheel spindle and fork top bolts. Pump forks several times, then retighten from bottom upwards.
	Fork legs bent	Replace legs.
Machine wanders. Steering imprecise, rear wheel tends to hop.	Worn swinging arm pivot	Dismantle and replace bushes and pivot pin.

Chapter 5 Wheels, Brakes and Final Drive

Contents

Specifications

Tyres
Front ... ...   3.25 x 19 in all models
Rear ... ...   4.00 x 18 in all models

Brakes
Front ... ...   Twin leading shoe drum brake
Rear ... ...   Conventional drum brake

Chain
Number of rollers ... ...   112 - 110

Note: Conversion kits are available for converting to British chain sizes. It is necessary to change the chain and both sprockets.

Tyre pressures
Front ... ...   23 psi
Rear (solo) ... ...   27 psi
Rear (with pillion rider) ... ...   33 psi

Final drive engine sprocket
Options - No of teeth 13, 14, 15

Rear sprocket
Options - No of teeth 33, 34, 35, 38, 39

1 General description

All models employ steel wheel rims in conjunction with cast, aluminium alloy hubs. Each wheel has, as standard, an 8 inch diameter internal expanding brake; the front brake is of the twin leading shoe type.

The front wheel carries a 3.25 x 19 inch ribbed tread tyre and the rear wheel has a 4.0 x 18 inch block tread tyre. (The tyres should be of a 4 ply rating.)

Both wheels are quickly detachable; the rear wheel can be removed from the frame without disturbing either the rear wheel sprocket or the final drive chain.

2 Front wheel - examination and renovation

1. Place the machine on the centre stand so that the front wheel is raised clear of the ground. Spin the wheel and check the rim alignment. Small irregularities can be corrected by tightening the spokes in the affected area, although a certain amount of experience is advisable to prevent over-correction. Any flats in the wheel rim should be evident at the same time. These are more difficult to remove and in most cases it will be necessary to have the wheel rebuilt on a new rim. Apart from the effect on stability, a flat will expose the tyre bead and walls to greater risk of damage if the machine is run with a deformed wheel.

2 Check for loose and broken spokes. Tapping the spokes is the best guide to tension. A loose spoke will produce a quite different sound and should be tightened by turning the nipple (right hand thread). Always recheck for run-out by spinning the wheel again. If the spokes have to be tightened an excessive amount, it is advisable to remove the tyre and tube, as detailed in Section 13 of this Chapter, so that the protruding ends of the spokes can be ground off in order to prevent them from chafing the inner tube and causing punctures.

3 Front brake assembly - examination, renovation and reassembly

All models except GT500A

1 The front brake assembly complete with brake plate can be withdrawn from the front wheel hub after the wheel spindle has been pulled out and the wheel removed from the forks. Refer to Chapter 4, Section 2.6 for the correct procedure.
2 Examine the condition of the brake linings. If they are wearing thin or unevenly the brake shoes should be replaced. The linings are bonded on and cannot be supplied separately.

3.2 The twin leading shoe brake assembly. Note the two brake operating cams

3 To remove the brake shoes, turn the brake operating lever so that the brake is in the fully on position. Pull the brake shoes apart to free them from the operating cams after releasing the pivot pins from the fixed ends, and lift them away complete with their return springs by reverting to a V formation. When they are well clear of the brake plate, the return springs can be removed and the shoes separated.
4 Before replacing the brake shoes, check that both brake operating cams are working smoothly and not binding in their pivots. The cams are removed for greasing by detaching their operating arm from the splined end of each shaft, after first slackening the pinch bolts. Before the arms are pulled off their respective shafts, mark their position on the splines to aid correct location. Do not alter the setting of the screwed rod which joins both arms, otherwise the brake setting will require re-adjustment after reassembly.
5 Check the inner surface of the brake drum on which the brake shoes bear. The surface should be smooth and free from score marks or indentations, otherwise reduced braking efficiency will be inevitable. Remove all traces of brake lining dust and wipe with a rag soaked in petrol to remove all traces of grease or oil. NEVER use paraffin for cleaning drums as its oily base will provide lubrication!
6 To reassemble the brake shoes on the brake plate, replace the return springs and pull the shoes apart, holding them in a V formation. If they are now located with the brake operating cams and pivots they can be pushed back into position by pressing downwards. Do not use excessive force, or there is risk of distorting the shoes permanently.
7 See Section 14 of this Chapter for information on the front

wheel disc brake fitted to the GT500A model.

4 Front wheel bearings - examination and replacement

1 Access is available to the wheel bearings when the brake plate has been removed. The left hand wheel bearing is exposed when the brake plate is lifted away; it is protected by an oil seal (when the brake plate is reassembled) which remains captive with the brake plate.
2 Lay the wheel on the ground, with the brake drum uppermost and with a drift of the correct diameter, drive out the distance piece which fits within the centre of the left hand wheel bearing. If this distance piece is driven to the right it will bring with it the right hand dust cover, spacer, oil seal and bearing. It will be necessary to support the wheel around the outer perimeter for these parts to be driven clear of the hub.
3 Invert the wheel and drive out the left hand bearing, using a larger diameter drift.
4 Remove all the old grease from the hub and bearings, giving the latter a final wash in petrol. Check the bearings for play or signs of roughness when they are turned. If there is any doubt about their condition, replace them.
5 Before replacing the bearings, first pack the hub with new grease. Then drive them back into position with the same drifts, not forgetting the distance piece which is located between the two bearing centres. Fit the replacement oil seal in front of the bearing on the right hand side, also the spacer and dust cover.
6 A somewhat similar arrangement is used for the GT500A model, but there is no brake plate to remove.

5 Front wheel - reassembly and replacement

1 Place the front brake plate and brake assembly in the brake drum and align the wheel between the forks so that the slot in the brake plate engages with the projection on the lower left hand fork leg. This acts as the anchorage for the front brake plate.
2 Align the wheel so that the front wheel spindle can be inserted from the right. It may be necessary to spring apart the bottom fork legs a small amount, so that the boss of the hub will locate with the lower right hand fork leg. Push the spindle home and screw it into the left hand fork leg, using a spanner across the end flats, until the spindle is fully tightened. Lock the spindle in position by retightening the clamp bolt through the lower right hand fork leg.
3 Spin the wheel to check that it moves freely, then attach the speedometer drive cable and the front brake cable. Check that the brake functions correctly, particularly if the brake operating arms have been removed and replaced. If necessary, re-adjust the brake by following the procedure described in Section 9 of this Chapter.

6 Rear wheel - examination, removal and renovation

1 Place the machine on the centre stand, so that the rear wheel is raised clear of the ground. Check for rim alignment, damage to the rim and loose or broken spokes by following the procedure relating to the front wheel in Section 2.
2 To remove the rear wheel, use the procedure recommended in Section 10.3 of Chapter 4, or, if there is no necessity to disturb either the rear sprocket or the final drive chain, an amended procedure as follows:
3 Detach the rear brake torque arm from the brake plate by removing the spring clip and withdrawing the securing nut, washer and bolt. Remove also the rear brake cable by unscrewing the adjuster and freeing the cable from the rear brake plate. Then withdraw the wheel from the sprocket and chain assembly by unscrewing the inner of the two left hand wheel nuts and removing the spindle. When the right hand distance piece is removed, there will be sufficient clearance for the wheel to be disengaged from the shock absorber vanes of the sprocket, and pulled clear from the frame.
4 The rear brake plate and brake assembly can be withdrawn from the right hand side of the wheel hub.
5 The rear wheel bearings are also a drive fit in the hub,

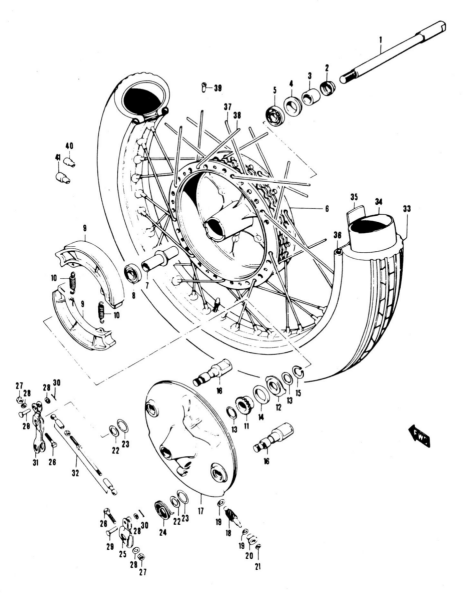

FIG. 5.1. FRONT WHEEL

1	Front wheel spindle
2	Dust cover
3	Wheel spindle spacer
4	Right hand oil seal
5	Right hand wheel bearing
6	Front hub and brake drum
7	Hub bearing spacer
8	Left hand wheel bearing
9	Brake shoe (2 off)
10	Brake shoe retaining spring (2 off)
11	Speedometer drive gear
12	Speedometer dog drive
13	Thrust washer (2 off)
14	Left hand oil seal
15	Circlip - speedo drive assembly
16	Brake cam and shaft (2 off)
17	Brake panel
18	Speedometer drive worm
19	Worm drive thrust washer (2 off)
20	Speedometer worm bush
21	Worm shaft oil seal
22	Thrust washer (2 off)
23	'O' ring brake cam (2 off)
24	Brake cam return spring
25	Secondary brake lever
26	Brake lever pinch bolt (2 off)
27	Nut (2 off)
28	Washer (4 off)
29	Clevis pin (2 off)
30	Split pin (2 off)
31	Primary brake lever
32	Brake lever connecting rod assembly
33	Tyre
34	Inner tube
35	Rim tape
36	Wheel rim
37	Spoke - inner (18 off)
38	Spoke - outer (18 off)
39	Spoke nipple (36 off)
40	Balance weight - short
41	Balance weight - long

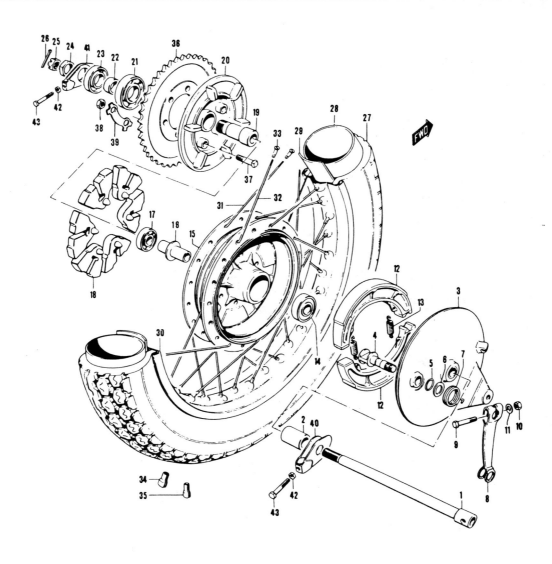

FIG. 5.2. REAR WHEEL

1	Rear wheel spindle	23	Sprocket bearing oil seal
2	Wheel spindle spacer	24	Sprocket bearing shaft nut
3	Rear brake plate	25	Castellated wheel spindle nut
4	Brake cam and shaft	26	Split pin
5	Brake cam 'O' ring seal	27	Rear tyre
6	Brake cam washer	28	Inner tube
7	Brake cam return spring	29	Rim tape
8	Brake lever	30	Wheel rim
9	Brake lever pinch bolt	31	Spoke - inner (18 off)
10	Nut	32	Spoke - outer (18 off)
11	Washer	33	Spoke nipple (36 off)
12	Rear brake shoe (2 off)	34	Balance weight - short
13	Brake shoe retaining spring (2 off)	35	Balance weight - long
14	Right hand wheel bearing	36	Rear sprocket
15	Rear hub and brake drum	37	Rear sprocket retaining bolts (6 off)
16	Hub bearing spacer	38	Nut (6 off)
17	Left hand wheel bearing	39	Sprocket tab washers (3 off)
18	Cush drive rubbers (6 off)	40	Right hand chain adjuster
19	Sprocket bearing shaft	41	Left hand chain adjuster
20	Sprocket/cush drive plate	42	Drawbolt locknut (2 off)
21	Sprocket shaft bearing	43	Chain adjuster drawbolt (2 off)
22	Sprocket shaft spacer		

separated by a spacer. Use a similar technique for removing, greasing and replacing the bearings to that adopted for the front wheel (Section 8 of this Chapter).

7 Rear brake assembly - examination, renovation and reassembly

1   The rear brake assembly complete with brake plate can be withdrawn from the rear wheel after the wheel spindle has been pulled out, the distance piece removed and the wheel pulled clear of the rear forks. The preceding section describes a simplified method of wheel removal if the wheel alone is to be removed.
2   If it is necessary to dismantle the rear brake assembly, follow the procedure described in Section 3 of this Chapter which applies to the front wheel. Note that the rear brake is of the single leading shoe type and therefore differs slightly in construction.
3   If the rear brake shoes are to be replaced, check carefully the condition of the operating cam and replace it if any signs of wear are apparent.

8 Adjusting the twin leading shoe front brake

1   If the front brake adjustment is correct, there should be a clearance of not less than 0.8 to 1.2 inch (20 to 30 mm) between the brake lever and the twist grip when the brake is applied fully.
2   Adjustment is effected by turning the adjuster nut in the end of the handlebar lever inwards to increase the clearance and outwards to decrease the clearance, or vice-versa, if the adjuster on the longer of the two brake operating arms is used.
3   The screwed operating rod which joins the two brake operating arms of the front brake should not require attention

8.1 The left hand wheel bearing is exposed when the brake plate is lifted away

unless the setting has been disturbed. It is imperative that the leading edge of each brake shoe comes into contact with the brake drum simultaneously, if maximum braking efficiency is to be achieved. Check by detaching the clevis pin from the eye of one end of the threaded rod, so that the brake operating arms can be applied independently. Operate each arm at a time and note when the brake shoe first commences to touch the brake drum, with the wheel spinning. Make a mark to show the exact position of each operating arm when this initial contact is made. Replace the clevis pin and check that the marks correspond when the brake is applied in similar fashion. If they do not, withdraw the clevis pin and use the adjuster to either increase or decrease the length of the rod until the marks correspond exactly. Replace the clevis pin and do not omit the split pin through the end which retains it in position. Recheck the brake lever adjustment before the machine is tried on the road.

4   Check that the brake pulls off correctly when the handlebar lever is released. Sluggish action is usually due to a poorly lubricated brake cable, broken return springs or a tendency for the brake operating cams to bind in their bushes. Dragging brakes affect engine performance and can cause severe overheating of both the brake shoes and wheel bearings.
5   The front disc brake fitted to the GT500A model is self-compensating and requires no adjustment

9 Adjusting the rear brake

1   If the adjustment of the rear brake is correct, the brake pedal will have a travel of from 0.8 to 1.2 inch (20 to 30 mm). Before the amount of travel is adjusted, the brake pedal position should be set so that the pedal is in the best position for quick operation.
2   The height of the brake pedal is determined by the adjuster at the end of the brake cable, where it joins the pedal arm. If the adjuster is screwed inwards, the pedal height is raised and vice-versa.
3   The length of travel is controlled by the adjuster at the end of the brake lever. If the nut is screwed inwards, travel is decreased and vice-versa.
4   Note that it may be necessary to re-adjust the height of the stop lamp switch if the pedal height has been altered to any marked extent. Refer to Chapter 6 for further details.
GENERAL NOTE: An indication of well worn brake linings may be obtained by noting the angle between the brake arm and the operating cable, when the brake is in the ON position. If this angle is more than 90° then either the linings are nearing the end of their life, or the brake arm has been set up incorrectly on its splines.

10 Cush drive assembly - examination and renovation

1   The cush drive assembly is contained within the left hand side of the rear wheel hub. It comprises a set of synthetic rubber buffers housed within a series of vanes cast in the hub shell. A plate attached to the gear wheel sprocket has six cast-in dogs which engage with slots in these rubbers, when the wheel is replaced in the frame. The drive to the rear wheel is transmitted via these rubbers, which cushion any surges or roughness in the drive which would otherwise convey the impression of harshness.
2   Examine the rubbers for signs of damage or general deterioration. Replace the rubbers if there is any doubt about their condition; they are held in place by moulded-in pegs on the back which press through holes in the wheel hub shell.

9.1 The slot in the brake plate must engage with the anchorage on the left hand fork leg

9.2 Lock the spindle in position by retightening the clamp bolt through the lower right-hand fork leg

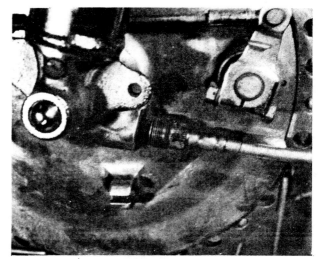

9.3a Replacing the speedometer drive cable ...

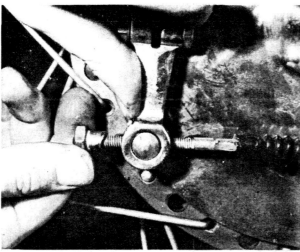

9.3b ... and front brake cable

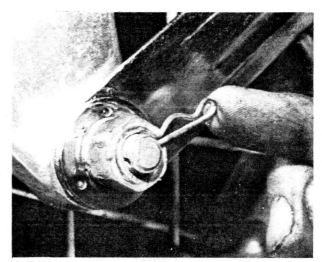

10.2a Detach the rear brake torque arm by removing the spring clip

10.2b ... and removing the securing nut, washer and bolt

10.2c Pull wheel to the right in order to disengage from the shock absorber vanes

10.3 The rear brake assembly withdrawn from the hub

11 Rear wheel sprocket - removal, examination and replacement

1 The rear wheel sprocket assembly can be removed as a separate unit after the rear wheel has been detached from the frame as described in Section 6.2 of this Chapter. Alternatively, it can be removed attached to the rear wheel if the procedure described in Section 10.3 of Chapter 4 is followed. In the latter case, the sprocket complete with the sprocket drum shaft and bearing will pull away from the cush drive when the wheel has been detached from the frame.

2 Check the condition of the sprocket teeth. If they are hooked, chipped or badly worn, the sprocket should be replaced. It is retained to the cush drive plate by six nuts and tab washers, which must be removed.

3 It is considered bad practice to replace one sprocket on its own. The final drive sprockets should always be renewed as a pair and a new chain fitted, otherwise rapid wear will necessitate even earlier replacement on the next occasion.

4 An additional bearing is located within the cush drive plate, which supports the sprocket drum shaft into which the rear wheel spindle fits. In common with the wheel bearings, this bearing is of the journal ball type and when wear occurs, the rear wheel sprocket will give the appearance of being slack on its mounting bolts. The bearing is a tight push fit on the sprocket drum shaft and is preceded by an oil seal which excludes road grit and water.

5 Remove the oil seal and bearing and wash out the latter to eliminate all traces of the old grease. If the bearing has any play or runs roughly, it must be replaced.

6 Prior to reassembly, the bearing should be repacked with grease and pushed back onto the shaft, followed by the oil seal. Replace the rear wheel assembly by reversing either of the methods adopted for its removal, whichever is appropriate.

12 Final drive chain - examination and lubrication

1 The final drive chain is fully exposed, with only a light chainguard over the top run. Periodically the tension will need to be re-adjusted, to compensate for wear. This is accomplished by slackening the inner and outer rear wheel nuts after the machine has been placed on the centre stand and drawing the wheel backwards by means of the draw bolt adjusters in the fork ends. The torque arm bolt on the rear brake plate must also be slackened during this operation.

2 The chain is in correct tension if there is from 0.6 to 0.8 inch (15 to 20 mm) of slack in the middle of the lower run. Always check when the chain is at its tightest point; a chain rarely wears evenly during service.

3 Always adjust the draw bolts an equal amount in order to preserve wheel alignment. The fork ends are marked with a series of horizontal lines above the adjusters, to provide a visual check. If desired, wheel alignment can be checked by running a plank of wood parallel to the machine, so that it touches both walls of the rear tyre. If wheel alignment is correct, it should be equidistant from either side of the front wheel tyre, when tested on both sides of the rear wheel. It will not touch the front wheel tyre because this tyre is of smaller cross section. See accompanying diagram.

4 Do not run the chain overtight to compensate for uneven wear. A tight chain will place excessive stresses on the gearbox and rear wheel bearings, leading to their early failure. It will also absorb a surprising amount of power.

5 After a period of running, the chain will require lubrication. Lack of oil will accelerate wear of both chain and sprockets and lead to harsh transmission. The application of engine oil will act as a temporary expedient, but it is preferable to remove the chain and immerse it in a molten lubricant such as Linklyfe or Chainguard, after it has been cleaned in a paraffin bath. These latter lubricants achieve better penetration of the chain links and rollers and are less likely to be thrown off when the chain is in motion.

6 To check whether the chain requires replacement initially, take up the slack from the chain with your left hand and try to pull the chain from the sprocket, radially, with your right hand. If there is any significant movement, remove the chain and lay it lengthwise in a straight line and compress it endwise until all the play is taken up. Anchor one end and pull on the other in order to take up the end play in the opposite direction. If the chain extends by more than the distance between two adjacent rollers, it should be replaced in conjunction with the sprockets. Note that this check should be made AFTER the chain has been washed out, but before any lubricant is applied, otherwise the lubricant will take up some of the play.

7 When replacing the chain, make sure the spring link is seated correctly, with the closed end facing the direction of travel.

13 Tyres - removal and replacement

1 At some time or other the need will arise to remove and replace the tyres, either as the result of a puncture or because a replacement is required to offset wear. To the inexperienced, tyre changing represents a formidable task yet if a few simple rules are observed and the technique learned, the whole operation is surprisingly simple.

2 To remove the tyre from either wheel, first detach the wheel from the machine by following the procedure in Chapter 4, Section 2.6 or Section 6.2 of this Chapter, depending on whether the front or the rear wheel is involved. Deflate the tyre by removing the valve insert and when it is fully deflated, push the bead of the tyre away from the wheel rim on both sides so that the bead enters the centre well of the rim. Remove the locking cap and push the tyre valve into the tyre itself.

3 Insert a tyre lever close to the valve and lever the edge of the tyre over the outside of the wheel rim. Very little force should be necessary; if resistance is encountered it is probably due to the fact that the tyre beads have not entered the well of the wheel rim all the way round the tyre.

4 Once the tyre has been edged over the wheel rim, it is easy to work around the wheel rim so that the tyre is completely free on one side. At this stage, the inner tube can be removed.

5 Working from the other side of the wheel, ease the other edge of the tyre over the outside of the wheel rim which is furthest away. Continue to work around the rim until the tyre is free completely from the rim.

6 If a puncture has necessitated the removal of the tyre, re-inflate the inner tube and immerse it in a bowl of water to trace the source of the leak. Mark its position and deflate the tube. Dry the tube and clean the area around the puncture with a petrol-soaked rag. When the surface has dried, apply the rubber solution and allow this to dry before removing the backing from

13.2 The adjuster at the end of the brake cable

necessary to use a tyre lever during the final stages.

12 Make sure there is no pull on the tyre valve and again commencing with the area furthest from the valve, ease the other bead of the tyre over the edge of the rim. Finish with the area close to the valve, pushing the valve up into the tyre until the locking cap touches the rim. This will ensure the inner tube is not trapped when the last section of the bead is edged over the rim with a tyre lever.

13 Check that the inner tube is not trapped at any point. Re-inflate the inner tube, and check that the tyre is seating correctly around the wheel rim. There should be a thin rib moulded around the wall of the tyre on both sides, which should be equidistant from the wheel rim at all points. If the tyre is unevenly located on the rim, try bouncing the wheel when the tyre is at the recommended pressure. It is probable that one of the beads has not pulled clear of the centre well.

14 Always run the tyres at the recommended pressures and never under or over inflate. The correct pressures for solo use are 23 psi front and 27 psi rear. If a pillion passenger is carried, increase the rear tyre pressure only to 33 psi.

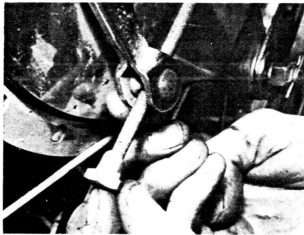

13.3 ... the adjuster at the end of the brake lever

14.1 The cush drive assembly within the rear hub

the patch and applying the patch to the surface.

7   It is best to use a patch of the self-vulcanising type, which will form a very permanent repair. Note that it may be necessary to remove a protective covering from the top surface of the patch, after it has sealed in position. Inner tubes made from synthetic rubber may require a special type of patch and adhesive, if a satisfactory bond is to be achieved.

8   Before replacing the tyre, check the inside to make sure the agent which caused the puncture is not trapped. Check also the outside of the tyre, particularly the tread area, to make sure nothing is trapped that may cause a further puncture.

9   If the inner tube has been patched on a number of past occasions, or if there is a tear or large hole, it is preferable to discard it and fit a replacement. Sudden deflation may cause an accident, particularly if it occurs with the front wheel.

10 To replace the tyre, inflate the inner tube sufficiently for it to assume a circular shape but only just. Then put it into the tyre so that it is enclosed completely. Lay the tyre on the wheel at an angle and insert the valve through the rim tape and the hole in the wheel rim. Attach the locking cap on the first few threads, sufficient to hold the valve captive in its correct location.

11 Starting at the point furthest from the valve, push the tyre bead over the edge of the wheel rim until it is located in the central well. Continue to work around the tyre in this fashion until the whole of one side of the tyre is on the rim. It may be

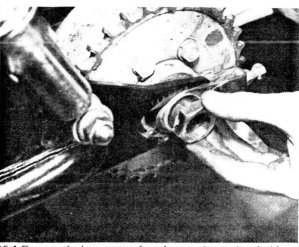

15.1 Remove the large nut to free the sprocket and cush drive plate

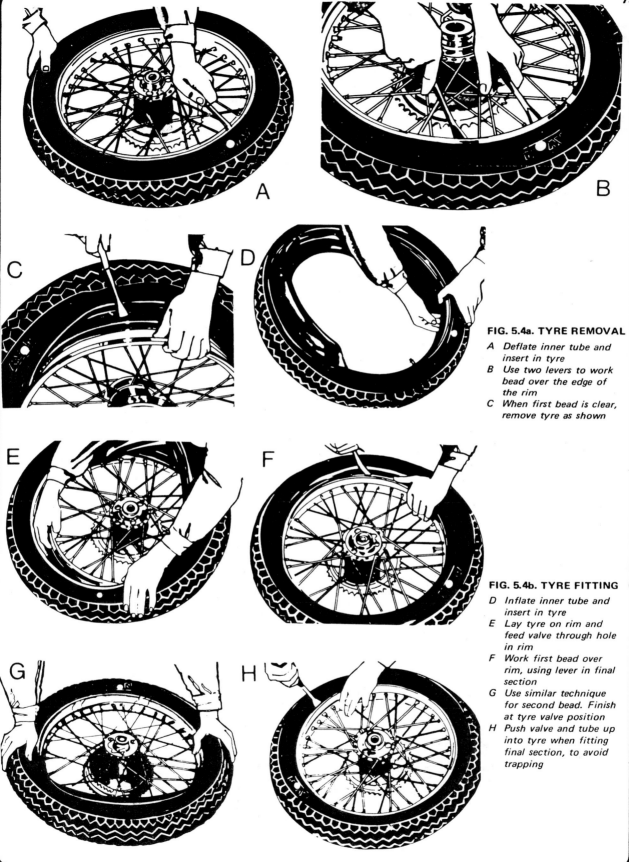

FIG. 5.4a. TYRE REMOVAL

A Deflate inner tube and insert in tyre
B Use two levers to work bead over the edge of the rim
C When first bead is clear, remove tyre as shown

FIG. 5.4b. TYRE FITTING

D Inflate inner tube and insert in tyre
E Lay tyre on rim and feed valve through hole in rim
F Work first bead over rim, using lever in final section
G Use similar technique for second bead. Finish at tyre valve position
H Push valve and tube up into tyre when fitting final section, to avoid trapping

15 Tyre replacement is aided by dusting the side walls, particularly in the vicinity of the beads, with a liberal coating of French chalk. Washing-up liquid can also be used to good effect, but this has the disadvantage of causing the inner surfaces of the wheel rim to rust.

16 Never replace the inner tube and tyre without the rim tape in position. If this precaution is overlooked there is good chance of the ends of the spoke nipples chafing the inner tube and causing a crop of punctures.

17 Never fit a tyre which has a damaged tread or side walls. Apart from the legal aspects, there is a very great risk of a blow-out which can have serious consequences on any two-wheel vehicle.

18 Tyre valves rarely give trouble, but it is always advisable to check whether the valve itself is leaking before removing the tyre. Do not forget to fit the dust cap, which forms an effective second seal.

14 Front wheel disc brake - examination and renovation

GT500A model only

1 Check the front brake master cylinder, hose and caliper unit for signs of fluid leakage. Pay particular attention to the condition of the hoses, which should be replaced without question if there are signs of cracking, splitting or other exterior damage.

2 Check also the level of hydraulic fluid by removing the cap on the brake fluid reservoir, diaphragm plate and diaphragm. This is one of the regular maintenance tasks, which should never be neglected. If the level is below the level mark, fluid of the correct grade must be added. NEVER USE ENGINE OIL or anything other than the recommended fluid. Other fluids have unsatisfactory characteristics and will rapidly destroy the seals.

3 The brake pads should also be inspected for wear. Each has a red line around its outer edge, which denotes the limit of wear. When this limit has been reached, BOTH pads must be replaced, even if only one has reached the limit line. Check by applying the brake so that the pads engage with the disc. They will lift out of the caliper unit when the front wheel is removed. See Section 5 of this Chapter.

4 If brake action becomes spongy, or if any part of the hydraulic system is dismantled (such as when the hose is replaced, for example), it is necessary to bleed the system in order to remove all traces of air. The following procedure should be followed:

1 Attach a tube to the bleed valve at the top of the caliper unit, after removing the dust cap. It is preferable to use a transparent plastics tube, so that the presence of air bubbles is seen more readily.

2 The far end of the tube should rest in a small bottle so that it is submerged in hydraulic fluid. This is essential, to prevent air from passing back into the system. In consequence, the end of the tube must remain submerged at all times.

3 Check that the reservoir on the handlebars is full of fluid and replace the cap to keep the fluid clean.

4 If spongy brake action necessitates the bleeding operation, squeeze and release the brake lever several times in rapid succession, to allow the pressure in the system to build up. Then open the bleed valve by unscrewing it one complete turn whilst maintaining pressure on the lever. This is a two-person operation. Squeeze the lever fully until it meets the handlebar, then close the bleed valve. If parts of the system have been replaced, the bleed valve can be opened from the beginning and the brake lever worked until fluid issues from the bleed tube. Note that it may be necessary to top up the reservoir during this operation; if it empties, air will enter the system and the whole operation will have to be repeated.

5 Repeat operation 4 until bubbles disappear from the bleed tube. Close the bleed valve fully, remove the bleed tube

and replace the dust cap.

6 Check the level in the reservoir and top up if necessary. Never use the fluid that has drained into the bottle at the end of the bleed tube because this contains air bubbles and will re-introduce air into the system. It must stand for 24 hours before it can be re-used.

7 Refit the diaphragm and diaphragm plate and tighten the reservoir cap securely.

8 Do not spill hydraulic fluid on the cycle parts. It is a very effective paint stripper!

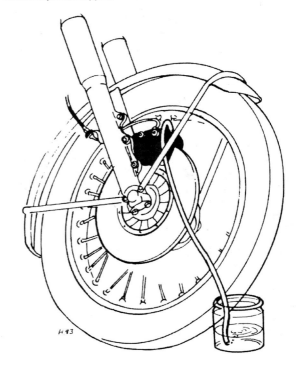

Fig. 5.5 Bleeding the front disc brake

15 Replacing the pads and overhauling the caliper unit

GT500 model only

1 Remove the front wheel by following the procedure described in Chapter 4, Section 2.6. Rotate the friction pads slightly and withdraw them from the caliper unit.

2 Inspect the friction pads closely and replace them both if the limit level of wear is approached, as described in paragraph 3 of the preceding Section. If there is any doubt whatsoever about their condition, they should be replaced as a pair.

3 Clean the recesses into which the pads fit and the exposed ends of the pistons that acutate them. Use only a small, soft brush and NOT solvent or a wire brush. Smear the piston faces and the brake pad recesses with hydraulic fluid, to act as a lubricant. Only sparing lubrication is required.

4 Remove the reservoir cap, diaphragm plate and diaphragm to check whether the level of fluid rises as the pistons are pushed back into the recesses. It may be necessary to syphon some fluid out of the reservoir prior to this operation, to prevent overflowing. If the pistons do not move freely, the caliper must be removed from the machine and overhauled. Because damage of some kind is inevitable the cause of piston seizures, it is best to entrust the repair of replacement of the unit to a Suzuki repair specialist.

16 Removing and replacing the disc

GT500A model only

1 It is unlikely that the disc will require attention unless it becomes badly scored and braking efficiency is reduced. The wear limit for disc thickness is 6 mm (0.236 in).

2 To remove the disc, first detach the front wheel complete from the forks, as described in Chapter 4, Section 2.6. The disc is bolted to the right-hand side of the wheel hub by six bolts, each pair having a common tab washer. Bend back the tab washer and remove the bolts, to release the disc.

3 Replace the disc by reversing the dismantling procedure. Make sure all the bolts are tightened fully and the tab washers are bent back into position.

17 Master cylinder - examination and renovation

GT500A model only

1 The master cylinder is unlikely to give trouble unless the machine has been stored for a lengthy period or until a considerable mileage has been covered. The usual signs of trouble are leakage of hydraulic fluid and a gradual fall in the fluid reservoir content.

2 To gain full access to the master cylinder, commence the dismantling operation by attaching a bleed tube to the caliper unit bleed nipple. Open the bleed nipple one complete turn, then operate the front brake lever until all fluid is pumped out of the reservoir. Close the bleed nipple, detach the tube and store the fluid in a closed container, for subsequent re-use.

3 Detach the hose and also the stop lamp switch (if fitted). Remove the handlebar lever pivot bolt and the lever itself.

4 Access is now available to the piston and the cylinder and it is possible to remove the piston assembly, together with all the relevant seals. Take note of the way in which the seals are arranged because they must be replaced in the same order. Failure to observe this necessity will result in brake failure.

5 Clean the master cylinder and piston with either hydraulic fluid or alcohol. On no account use either abrasives or other solvents such as petrol. If any signs of water or damage are evident, replacement is necessary. It is not practicable to reclaim either the piston or the cylinder bore.

6 Soak the new replacement seals in hydraulic fluid for about 15 minutes prior to replacement, then reassemble the parts IN EXACTLY THE SAME ORDER, using the reversal of the dismantling procedure. Lubricate with hydraulic fluid and make sure the feather edges of the various seals are not damaged.

7 Refit the assembled master cylinder unit to the handlebar, and reconnect the handlebar lever, hose, stop lamp etc. Refill the reservoir with hydraulic fluid and bleed the entire system by following the procedure detailed in Section 4.4 of this Chapter.

8 Check that the brake is working correctly before taking the machine on the road, to restore pressure and align the pads correctly. Use the brake gently for the first 50 miles or so to enable all the new parts to bed down correctly.

18 Fault diagnosis

Symptom	Reason/s	Remedy
Handlebars oscillate at low speeds	Buckled front wheel Incorrectly fitted front tyre	Remove wheel for specialist attention. Check whether line around bead is equidistant from rim.
Forks 'hammer' at high speeds	Front wheel out of balance	Add weights until wheel will stop in any position.
Brakes grab, locking wheel	Ends of brake shoes not chamfered	Remove brake shoes and chamfer ends.
Brakes feel spongy	Stretched brake operating cables, weak pull-off springs Air in hydraulic system (GT500A)	Replace cables and/or springs, after inspection. Bleed front brakes.
Tyres wear more rapidly in middle of tread	Over-inflation	Check pressures and run at recommended settings.
Tyres wear rapidly at outer edges of tread	Under-inflation	Check pressures and run at recommended settings.

Chapter 6 Electrical system

Contents

Specifications

Battery

Type	Lead acid
Make	Yuasa MBR3-12D
	Furukawa FB 12N7-4A
	Furukawa BRT3-12G
Voltage	12 volts
Capacity	7 amp hr

Alternator

Output	1.5 - 2.5 amps at 8000 rpm (daytime running - light electrical load)
	2 - 3 amps at 8000 rpm (night running - heavy electrical load)
Cut out	1500 rpm (day and night)
Main fuse	15 amp

Bulbs

Main headlamp	35/25W Pre-focus
Parking lamp	3.4W bayonet fitting
Tail/stop lamp	7/23W offset pins
Speedometer lamp	3.4W bayonet fitting
Tachometer lamp	3.4W bayonet fitting
Neutral indicator lamp	3.4W bayonet fitting
Headlamp beam indicator lamp	3.4W bayonet fitting
Flashing indicators lamp	1.7W bayonet fitting
Flashing indicator lamps	23W each bayonet fitting

All bulbs 12 volt rating

1 General description

The styling changes which exist between the various T500 models affect the layout of the headlamp and rear stop/tail lamp assemblies. These changes will not affect the appropriate stripdowns and procedures of this Chapter.

The 500 cc Suzuki twins are fitted with a 12 volt electrical system. The circuit comprises a crankshaft-driven rotating magnet alternator which has a stator with six coils, each pair coupled in series. During daytime running, only one set of coils is used because the only electrical demand is from the ignition circuit and the occasional use of the stop lamp. At night, all three sets of coils are used in order to meet the additional load of the lighting equipment. The coils work in parallel, to supply the extra current.

The output from the alternator is AC hence a rectifier is included in the circuit to convert this current to DC for charging the 12 volt, 7 amp hr battery. The daytime charging rate is within the 1.5 - 2.5 ampere range; at night the rate increases to within the 2 - 3 ampere range. These are the peak readings at 8000 rpm engine speed, measured at the positive (red) terminal of the battery. Note: If the machine is only used for short distances in winter and the battery goes flat quickly, an increased charging rate may be obtained by interchanging the green/white and green/red wires from the alternator at the snap connector entry (or exit). Do not forget to reverse the wires to their original position when use of the lights decreases, or the system will be damaged.

The charging of the battery is controlled by the voltage regulator. This unit is effectively a solid state relay which allows the battery to be charged at an approximately constant amperage and also protects the battery from high charging rates.

2 Crankshaft alternator - checking the output

As explained in Chapter 3, Section 2 the output from the alternator can be checked only with specialised test equipment of the multi-meter type. If the performance of the alternator is in any way suspect, it should be checked by either a Suzuki agent or an auto-electrical specialist.

3 Battery - inspection and maintenance

1 The battery is of the lead-acid type and has a capacity of 7 amp hrs.

2 The transparent case of the battery allows the upper and lower levels of the electrolyte to be observed without need to remove the battery. Maintenance is normally limited to keeping the electrolyte level between the prescribed upper and lower limits and making sure the vent tube is not blocked. The lead plates and their separators can be seen through the transparent case, a further guide to the condition of the battery; ie a charged battery has plates of a muddy brown colour; grey plates indicate a high level of sulphation and the battery should be replaced. If the battery case has sediment at the bottom, the plates are breaking up and the battery will soon need renewing.

3 Unless acid is spilt, as may occur if the machine falls over, the electrolyte should always be topped up with distilled water, to restore the correct level. If acid is spilt on any part of the machine, it should be neutralised with an alkali such as washing soda and washed away with plenty of water, otherwise serious corrosion will occur. Top up with sulphuric acid of the correct specific gravity (1.260 - 1.280) only when spillage has occurred. Check that the vent pipe is well clear of the frame tubes or any of the other cycle parts.

4 It is seldom practicable to repair a cracked battery case because the acid in the joint prevents the formation of an effective seal. It is always best to replace a cracked battery, especially in view of the corrosion which will be caused by acid leakage.

5 If the machine is laid up for a period, it is advisable to remove the battery and give it a 'refresher' charge every six weeks or so from a battery charger. If the battery is permitted to discharge completely, the plates will sulphate and render the battery useless.

4 Battery - charging procedure

1 The normal charging rate for the 7 amp hr battery fitted to the 500 cc Suzuki twins is 0.7 amps. A more rapid charge may be given in an emergency, in which case the charging rate may be increased to 1 amp. The higher charge rate should be avoided if possible as it will eventually shorten the working life of the battery.

2 Make sure the charger connections to the battery are correct; red to positive and black to negative. It is preferable to remove the battery from the machine during the charging operation and to remove the vent plug from each cell.

5 Silicon rectifier - general description

1 The function of the silicon rectifier is to convert the AC current produced by the alternator to DC so that it can be used to charge the battery. The rectifier is of the full wave type.

2 The rectifier is located in a position where it is not directly exposed to water or battery acid, which may cause it to malfunction. The question of access is of little importance because the rectifier is unlikely to give trouble during normal service. It is not practicable to repair a damaged rectifier. If the unit malfunctions, it must be replaced.

3 Damage to the rectifier will occur if the machine is run without the battery for any period of time. A high voltage will develop in the absence of any load on the electrical coils, which will cause a reverse flow of current and consequent damage to the rectifier cells. Reverse connection of the battery will also have the same effect.

4 It is not possible to check whether the rectifier is functioning correctly without the appropriate test equipment. A Suzuki agent or an auto-electrical specialist are best qualified to advise.

5 Do not loosen the rectifier locking nut, or in any way damage the surfaces of the assembly. Such action may cause the coating over the electrodes to peel and destroy the working action.

6 Fuse - location and replacement

1 A fuse is incorporated in the electrical system to give protection from a sudden over-load, as may occur during a short circuit. It is found within a fuse holder which forms part of the wiring snap connections, close to the battery. A transparent plastic bag attached to the wiring carries a spare fuse, for use in an emergency. The fuse is rated at 15 amps.

2 If a fuse blows, it should be replaced, after checking to ensure that no obvious short circuit has occurred. If the second fuse blows shortly afterwards, the electrical circuit must be checked thoroughly, to trace the fault.

3 When a fuse blows whilst the machine is running and no spare is available, a 'get you home' remedy is to remove the blown fuse and wrap it in silver paper before replacing it in the fuse holder. The silver paper will restore electrical continuity by bridging the broken fuse wire. This expedient should never be used if there is evidence of a short circuit or other major electrical fault, otherwise more serious damage will be caused. Replace the blown fuse at the earliest possible opportunity, to restore full circuit protection.

7 Headlamp - replacing bulbs and adjusting beam height

1 To remove the headlamp rim, detach the two small crosshead screws in the lower front portion of the headlamp shell - one near each fork leg. The headlamp rim can now be pulled away from the shell and lifted off when it has cleared the lip at the top.

2 The main bulb is of the double-filament type, to give a dipped beam facility. The bulb holder is attached to the reflector by a rubber sleeve, which fits around the flange in the reflector and the flange of the bulb holder itself. The bulb is rated at 12 volts, 35/25W.

3 It is not necessary to refocus the headlamp when a new bulb is fitted because the bulbs used are of the pre-focus type. To release the main headlamp bulb, press and twist it in the holder.

4 The pilot lamp bulb holder is a bayonet fitting in the reflector, below the main bulb. The bulb holder is protected by a rubber sleeve. Used for parking purposes only, the bulb has a 12 volt, 3W rating.

5 Beam alignment is adjusted by means of a small screw through the left hand side of the headlamp rim, just below the telescopic fork lug to which the headlamp shell is attached. The screw passes through a plate attached to the back of the reflector, into a threaded nylon insert. By turning the screw, the headlamp beam can be ranged to either the right or the left, in the horizontal plane.

6 Beam height is adjusted by slackening the two bolts which retain the headlamp shell in position (through the lugs from the telescopic forks) and tilting the shell either upwards or downwards before retightening.

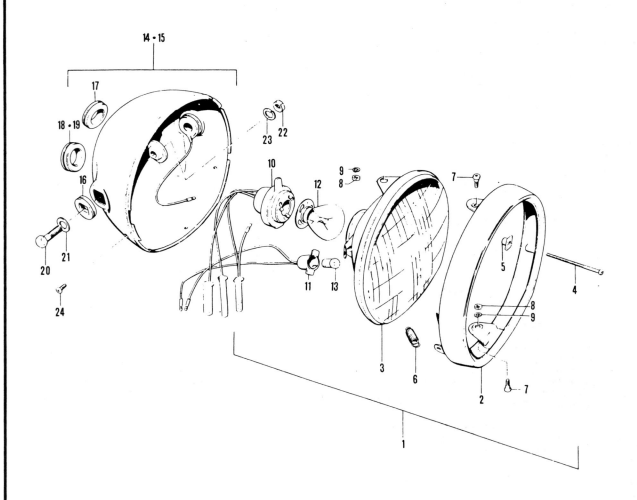

FIG. 6.1. HEADLAMP ASSEMBLY (EXCEPT T500K AND T500L MODELS

1	Headlamp assembly		14	Headlamp shell assembly - painted
2	Headlamp rim		15	Headlamp shell assembly - chromium plated
3	Reflector unit		16	Rubber spacer (2 off)
4	Beam adjusting screw		17	ID 28 mm
5	Beam adjusting screw nut		18	ID 20 mm
6	Bulb holder spring		19	ID 16 mm
7	Retaining screw (2 off)		20	Headlamp mounting bolt (2 off)
8	Nut (2 off)		21	Washer (2 off)
9	Spring washer (2 off)		22	Nut (2 off) *
10	Bulb holder - main bulb		23	Spring washer (2 off) *
11	Bulb holder - parking lamp		24	Rim retaining screw (2 off)
12	Headlamp main bulb			
13	Parking lamp bulb		*	On T500, T500R and T500J models only

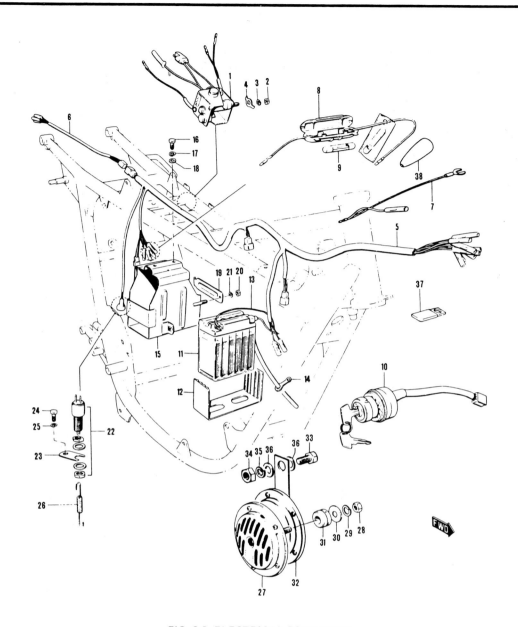

FIG. 6.2. ELECTRICAL EQUIPMENT

1	Rectifier assembly	21	Spring washer *
2	Nut	22	Stop lamp switch assembly
3	Spring washer	23	Stop lamp switch bracket
4	Rectifier lock washer	24	Bolt
5	Wiring harness	25	Spring washer
6	Rear wiring loom	26	Switch operating spring
7	Handlebar earth loom	27	Horn *
8	Fuse case assembly	28	Nut *
9	Main fuse	29	Spring washer *
10	Ignition switch assembly	30	Washer *
11	Battery	31	Cushion *
12	Battery cushion pad	32	Horn +
13	Battery cable	33	Bolt +
14	Battery vent pipe holder	34	But +
15	Battery holder	35	Spring washer +
16	Bolt (2 off)	36	Washer +
17	Spring washer (2 off)	37	Clamp (optional)
18	Washer	38	Fuse lead waterproof boot (optional)
19	Battery retaining plate *	*	T500 only
20	Nut *	+	All models except T500

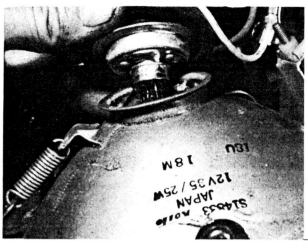

7.2 Main bulb is attached to reflector unit by a rubber sleeve

9.1 Remove lens cover for access to rear lamp bulb

7   To check the headlamp alignment, place the machine on level ground facing a wall 25 yards distant, with the rider seated normally. The height of the beam centre should be equal to that of the height of the centre of the headlamp from the ground, when the dip switch is in the 'fully on' position. The concentrated area of light should be centrally disposed. Adjustments in either direction are made as detailed in the preceding paragraphs. Note that a different setting for the beam height will be required when a pillion passenger is carried.

8   The above instructions for beam setting relate to the requirements of the United Kingdom's Transport Lighting Regulations. Other settings may be required in countries other than the UK.

8 Handlebar dipswitch - examination

The dipswitch forms part of the left hand 'dummy' twist grip and should not normally give trouble. In the event of failure, the switch assembly complete must be replaced; it is not practicable to effect a permanent repair.

9 Stop and tail lamp - replacing bulbs

1   The tail lamp has a twin filament bulb of 12 volt, 7/23W rating, to illuminate the rear number plate and to give visual warning when the rear brake is applied. To gain access to the bulb, remove the two screws which retain the moulded plastic lens cover to the tail lamp assembly, and remove the cover complete with gasket. The bulb has a bayonet fitting, with staggered pins to prevent the bulb contacts from being reversed.

2   If the tail lamp bulb keeps blowing, suspect either vibration in the rear mudguard assembly, or more probably, a poor earth connection.

3   The stop lamp is operated by a stop lamp switch on the right hand side of the machine, immediately above the brake pedal. It is connected to the pedal by an extension spring, which acts as the operating link. The body of the switch is threaded so that a limited range of adjustment is available, to determine when the lamp will operate.

10 Flashing indicators

1   The forward flashing indicator lamps are connected to 'stalks' which thread into the alloy top yoke of the telescopic forks. They are retained by a locknut and can be set to any level desired. The rear-facing indicator lamps are also mounted on stalks and thread through a metal plate attached to each side of the rear 'grab handle'.

2   In each case, access to the bulb is gained by removing the moulded plastic lens cover. Each bulb is rated at 12 volts, 23W.

10.2 Remove lens cover to gain access to flashing indicator bulb

11 Flasher unit - location and replacement

1   The flasher unit is bolted to the left hand side of the rectifier assembly, below and close to the nose of the dual seat.

2   A series of audible clicks will be heard if the flasher unit is functioning correctly. If the unit malfunctions, the usual symptom is one initial flash before the unit goes dead. It will be necessary to replace the flasher unit complete if the fault cannot be attributed to either a burnt out indicator bulb or a blown fuse. Take great care when handling the unit because it is easily damaged if dropped.

12 Tachometer head - replacement of bulbs

1   The tachometer head houses no less than four bulbs, each of which has an indicating function, apart from the bulb used for internal illumination. The indicating function and the bulb ratings are as follows:

Flashing indicator lamp	12 volt, 1.7W
Full headlamp beam indicator lamp	12 volt, 3.4W
Neutral indicator lamp	12 volt, 3.4W
Tachometer dial illumination lamp	12 volt, 3.4W

2   The bulb holders are a push fit into the base of the tachometer head, where they are retained by their outer

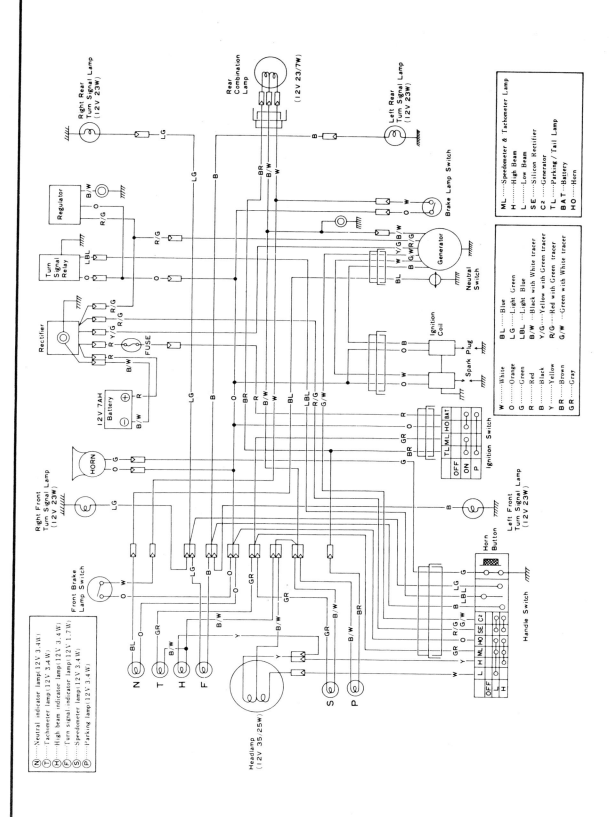

Fig. 6.3. Suzuki 500 Wiring diagram

moulded rubber sleeves. The bulbs have a bayonet fitting.

13 Speedometer head - replacement of bulb

1   The speedometer dial is illuminated by a 12 volt, 3.4W bulb which is a push fit into the base of the head, as in the case of the matching tachometer.
2   The speedometer illuminating bulb also has a bayonet fitting.

14 Horn - location and examination

1   The horn is suspended from a flexible steel strip mounted on the crossmember which joins the two front down tubes of the frame, immediately below the steering head. The flexible steel strip isolates the horn from the undesirable effects of high frequency vibration.
2   The horn has no external means of adjustment. If it malfunctions it must be replaced; it is a statutory requirement that the machine must be fitted with a horn which is in working order.

15 Wiring - layout and examination

1   The wiring harness is colour-coded and will correspond with the accompanying diagram. Where socket connectors are used, they are designed so that reconnection can be made only in the one correct position.
2   Visual inspection will show whether any breaks or frayed outer coverings are giving rise to short circuits. Another source of trouble may be the snap connectors and sockets, where the connector has not been pushed home fully in the outer housing.
3   Intermittent short circuits can often be traced to a chafed wire which passes through or is close to a metal component, such as a frame member. Avoid tight bends in the wire or situations where the wire can become trapped between casings.

16 Ignition and lighting switch

1   On early models the ignition and lighting switch is combined in one unit. It is operated by a key which cannot be removed when the ignition is switched on.
2   The number stamped on the key will match also the number of the steering head lock. A replacement key can be obtained if the number is quoted; if either lock or the ignition switch is changed extra keys will be needed.
3   It is not practicable to repair the ignition switch if it malfunctions. It should be replaced with a new lock and key to suit.
4   Later models have the ignition and lighting switches separate but working in conjunction with each other, ie the main lights are inoperative when the ignition switch is in the OFF or the PARK position.

17 Fault diagnosis

Symptom	Reason/s	Remedy
Complete electrical failure	Blown fuse	Check wiring and electrical components for short circuit before fitting new 15 amp fuse. Check battery connections, also whether connections show signs of corrosion.
Dim lights, horn inoperative	Discharged battery	Recharge battery with battery charger and check whether alternator is giving correct output (electrical specialist).
Constantly 'blowing' bulbs	Vibration, poor earth connection	Check whether bulb holders are secured correctly. Check earth return or connections to frame.

Metric conversion tables

Inches	Decimals	Millimetres
1/64	0.015625	0.3969
1/32	0.03125	0.7937
3/64	0.046875	1.1906
1/16	0.0625	1.5875
5/64	0.078125	1.9844
3/32	0.09375	2.3812
7/64	0.109375	2.7781
1/8	0.125	3.1750
9/64	0.140625	3.5719
5/32	0.15625	3.9687
11/64	0.171875	4.3656
3/16	0.1875	4.7625
13/64	0.203125	5.1594
7/32	0.21875	5.5562
15/64	0.234375	5.9531
1/4	0.25	6.3500
17/64	0.265625	6.7469
9/32	0.28125	7.1437
19/64	0.296875	7.5406
5/16	0.3125	7.9375
21/64	0.328125	8.3344
11/32	0.34375	8.7312
23/64	0.359375	9.1281
3/8	0.375	9.5250
25/64	0.390625	9.9219
13/32	0.40625	10.3187
27/64	0.421875	10.7156
7/16	0.4375	11.1125
29/64	0.453125	11.5094
15/32	0.46875	11.9062
31/64	0.484375	12.3031
1/2	0.5	12.7000
33/64	0.515625	13.0969
17/32	0.53125	13.4937
35/64	0.546875	13.8906
9/16	0.5625	14.2875
37/64	0.578125	14.6844
19/32	0.59375	15.0812
39/64	0.609375	15.4781
5/8	0.625	15.8750
41/64	0.640625	16.2719
21/32	0.65625	16.6687
43/64	0.671875	17.0656
11/16	0.6875	17.4625
45/64	0.703125	17.8594
23/32	0.71875	18.2562
47/64	0.734375	18.6531
3/4	0.75	19.0500
49/64	0.765625	19.4469
25/32	0.78125	19.8437
51/64	0.796875	20.2406
13/16	0.8125	20.6375
53/64	0.828125	21.0344
27/32	0.84375	21.4312
55/64	0.859375	21.8281
7/8	0.875	22.2250
57/64	0.890625	22.6219
29/32	0.90625	23.0187
59/64	0.921875	23.4156
15/16	0.9375	23.8125
61/64	0.953125	24.2094
31/32	0.96875	24.6062
63/64	0.984375	25.0031

Millimetres to Inches	
mm	Inches
0.01	0.00039
0.02	0.00079
0.03	0.00118
0.04	0.00157
0.05	0.00197
0.06	0.00236
0.07	0.00276
0.08	0.00315
0.09	0.00354
0.1	0.00394
0.2	0.00787
0.3	0.01181
0.4	0.01575
0.5	0.01969
0.6	0.02362
0.7	0.02756
0.8	0.03150
0.9	0.03543
1	0.03937
2	0.07874
3	0.11811
4	0.15748
5	0.19685
6	0.23622
7	0.27559
8	0.31496
9	0.35433
10	0.39370
11	0.43307
12	0.47244
13	0.51181
14	0.55118
15	0.59055
16	0.62992
17	0.66929
18	0.70866
19	0.74803
20	0.78740
21	0.82677
22	0.86614
23	0.90551
24	0.94488
25	0.98425
26	1.02362
27	1.06299
28	1.10236
29	1.14173
30	1.18110
31	1.22047
32	1.25984
33	1.29921
34	1.33858
35	1.37795
36	1.41732
37	1.4567
38	1.4961
39	1.5354
40	1.5748
41	1.6142
42	1.6535
43	1.6929
44	1.7323
45	1.7717

Inches to Millimetres	
Inches	mm
0.001	0.0254
0.002	0.0508
0.003	0.0762
0.004	0.1016
0.005	0.1270
0.006	0.1524
0.007	0.1778
0.008	0.2032
0.009	0.2286
0.01	0.254
0.02	0.508
0.03	0.762
0.04	1.016
0.05	1.270
0.06	1.524
0.07	1.778
0.08	2.032
0.09	2.286
0.1	2.54
0.2	5.08
0.3	7.62
0.4	10.16
0.5	12.70
0.6	15.24
0.7	17.78
0.8	20.32
0.9	22.86
1	25.4
2	50.8
3	76.2
4	101.6
5	127.0
6	152.4
7	177.8
8	203.2
9	228.6
10	254.0
11	279.4
12	304.8
13	330.2
14	355.6
15	381.0
16	406.4
17	431.8
18	457.2
19	482.6
20	508.0
21	533.4
22	558.8
23	584.2
24	609.6
25	635.0
26	660.4
27	685.8
28	711.2
29	736.6
30	762.0
31	787.4
32	812.8
33	838.2
34	863.6
35	889.0
36	914.4

English/American terminology

Because this book has been written in England, British English component names, phrases and spellings have been used throughout. American English usage is quite often different and whereas normally no confusion should occur, a list of equivalent terminology is given below.

English	American	English	American
Air filter	Air cleaner	Mudguard	Fender
Alignment (headlamp)	Aim	Number plate	License plate
Allen screw/key	Socket screw/wrench	Output or layshaft	Countershaft
Anticlockwise	Counterclockwise	Panniers	Side cases
Bottom/top gear	Low/high gear	Paraffin	Kerosene
Bottom/top yoke	Bottom/top triple clamp	Petrol	Gasoline
Bush	Bushing	Petrol/fuel tank	Gas tank
Carburettor	Carburetor	Pinking	Pinging
Catch	Latch	Rear suspension unit	Rear shock absorber
Circlip	Snap ring	Rocker cover	Valve cover
Clutch drum	Clutch housing	Selector	Shifter
Dip switch	Dimmer switch	Self-locking pliers	Vise-grips
Disulphide	Disulfide	Side or parking lamp	Parking or auxiliary light
Dynamo	DC generator	Side or prop stand	Kick stand
Earth	Ground	Silencer	Muffler
End float	End play	Spanner	Wrench
Engineer's blue	Machinist's dye	Split pin	Cotter pin
Exhaust pipe	Header	Stanchion	Tube
Fault diagnosis	Trouble shooting	Sulphuric	Sulfuric
Float chamber	Float bowl	Sump	Oil pan
Footrest	Footpeg	Swinging arm	Swingarm
Fuel/petrol tap	Petcock	Tab washer	Lock washer
Gaiter	Boot	Top box	Trunk
Gearbox	Transmission	Two/four stroke	Two/four cycle
Gearchange	Shift	Tyre	Tire
Gudgeon pin	Wrist/piston pin	Valve collar	Valve retainer
Indicator	Turn signal	Valve collets	Valve cotters
Inlet	Intake	Vice	Vise
Input shaft or mainshaft	Mainshaft	Wheel spindle	Axle
Kickstart	Kickstarter	White spirit	Stoddard solvent
Lower leg	Slider	Windscreen	Windshield

Index